Gerardo Castillo

TEENAGERS AND THEIR PROBLEMS

GERARDO CASTILLO

Teenagers
and their problems

FOUR COURTS PRESS

The typesetting for this book was keyboarded by Gilbert
Gough Typesetters, Dublin, and output in 10.5 on 12pt
Plantin by Computer Graphics Ltd, Dublin, for Four
Courts Press Ltd, Kill Lane, Blackrock, Co. Dublin.

ISBN 1-85182-012-4 pbk
ISBN 1-85182-013-2 hbk

Printed in Great Britain by
Richard Clay (The Chaucer Press) Ltd,
Bungay, Suffolk

Contents

Introduction

My main purpose in writing this book is to help parents to achieve one particular objective which must be of prime concern to them, namely to get to know their teenage children.

If we know our children, we can understand their behaviour. We can see the difference, for instance, between a passing phase or something that happens just once and something more permanent or relatively constant in their conduct; we can distinguish between their intention and the way they outwardly show how they feel. One and the same way of behaving may stem from different causes; it may mean different things in each child or at each particular time or depending on the situation.

We really do need to get to know our children if their upbringing is to make sense. If they are to be educated properly, each must be pointed in the right direction, according to his or her abilities, limitations and specific needs. The same objectives will not suit them all, for they are all different from one another. Only when we know them, at least reasonably well, can we hope to see whether they are making any real progress, and, if so, whether they are making enough progress; only then can we make demands on them or guide them along lines suitable to their particular abilities. If, on the other hand, we try to influence them without getting to know or understand them, we will find it impossible to set them valid or realistic goals, impossible to know whether we are getting anywhere and impossible to direct and advise them properly, for guidance must always be fitted to the personal qualities of the particular individual. Anyone who hopes to help a child to mature must first get to know and accept him for what he is: otherwise success will evade even his best efforts.

Every child is the way he is by reason of three factors: sex, personality and age or degree of maturity. He differs, not only from adults (both quantitatively and qualitatively, so to speak), but also from all other children of the same age and even from himself or herself from one stage to another. These differences are especially

7

significant in this most important phase of his development, namely adolescence. When he goes through this phase, not only is he different, but he is actually discovering these differences for the first time, becoming aware of his own intimacy and identity and growing interested in preserving and defending them.

The real significance of this phase has been discovered relatively recently. M. Débesse calls it "the Cinderella of life's various stages" and compares it with Poland, unhappily poised between two powerful neighbours: "It is neither the end of childhood nor is it the adulthood in embryo, but a phase in its own right, with a value of its own . . . It is not just one more phase in our life, but a complete and complex reality: a world in itself".[1] It is a time of discovery, a time for discovering oneself and others, a time for broadening one's horizons.

In a sense we could say that all education refers to adolescence because our understanding of this age also helps us to guide younger children on the way towards it and to help adults with adolescent fixations. When Débesse tells parents that they have more than one adolescent in their household, he undoubtedly means that there is no radical break between the last stage of childhood — from seven to ten years of age approximately — and puberty; many children reach puberty while still in that final stage of childhood. Even the middle stage of childhood, from three to seven, has curious similarities with puberty: for example, irritability and stubbornness in imposing one's own wishes. Henry Wallon finds in this stage the first expressions of one's sense of personality.

Not only does adolescence tend to begin earlier than usually realized, but it also continues much later than at first appears to be the case. T. A. Jersild writes: "One important reason for studying adolescence may be that we wish to learn something about ourselves: whatever our age, much of our adolescence remains in us. Anything that helps us to get to grips with the teenager we once were will give us a better understanding of the type of person we now are".[2] Adolescence, in fact, extends into the years of adulthood, both in its positive and in its negative features, a tendency to blame others, a desire to separate "body" and "soul", emotional problems, inability to see anything but black and white, indiscriminate rebellion . . . Hopefully a study of this phase may also help to change for the better the "adolescent" consumer society we live in — pragmatic, permissive and comfort-living.

These very characteristics of present-day society make it difficult to give teenagers the guidance they need. Indeed, it may well be true that the worst part of the crisis among young people today is that our society is not only incapable of relieving their emotional helplessness and insecurity, but it actually aggravates it.[3] The tendency to manipulate people (through advertising, in sexual matters and questions of right and wrong) has greatly magnified this problem and shows that nowadays it is no longer sufficient, as it might have been in the past, to rely on the example and good habits learned in the home, in order to face up to life in a responsible manner, although of course such lessons are still important. Unfortunately there are more and more cases of youngsters who have been well brought up in the home but who run wild at the age of thirteen or fourteen and, for example, become drop-outs, juvenile delinquents or drug addicts.

These reasons alone explain why the whole subject of teenagers and adolescents is talked about so much nowadays. Parents, family counsellors and indeed everyone involved in education must realize the importance of adolescence today and they should prepare children from an early age to meet the crisis with a solid background behind them so as to avoid the numerous dangers that await them.[4] More than ever before, there is a need for preventative measures to be taken against the negative influence of the environment.

Parents should also be aware that they are responsible to a great extent for determining whether their children's adolescence will be problem-free or not. The important thing is that they should try to get to know and understand them, encouraging positive attitudes which will help them to overcome the crisis. Regrettably we have to say that in many families there is insufficient knowledge on the whole question of adolescence. To be fair, we must add that it is by no means easy to get to know teenagers; they are at an age which is closed and secret, which evades questions or gives scarcely creditable answers; it is also a time of change; their behaviour may disconcert even an expert observer. It is an age closed in upon itself (Débesse, 27). Nor must we forget that "from adolescence on, when a person takes it on himself to be, not just a separate being, but a distinct and free person, the individual's personality ceases to be relatively patent. It is his and his alone; his own intimacy is therefore basically impenetrable"[5] (M. Yela).

Far from being insurmountable obstacles, however, the difficulties involved in getting to know their teenage children should offer parents a challenge and a stimulus. The difficulties will diminish if a lot is expected of the children, if there is a confidence in their potential, if there is an atmosphere of trust and acceptance in which they and their parents grow and mature together. Apart from the difficulty of getting to know them, parents also find that sometimes children refuse to accept help. The teenager is a rebel but not a self-sufficient one; he is immature and suffers from a peculiar paradox: just when he is most in need of help, he refuses it because he is afraid of returning to the subjection of his earlier childhood. The problem becomes even more acute when the parent tries to think for the child or attempts to help without first having stimulated a desire to ask for such help.

At every stage of children's development we have to encourage their self-sufficiency, but this is particularly necessary in the case of teenagers, because they need to be self-sufficient if they are to develop their own newly discovered personal identity. They must constantly look for opportunities to act on their own initiative and on their own responsibility, without their parents continually watching them. Parents ought to encourage this autonomy, this gradual separation, allowing children to take the risks involved in learning to act on their own. However, this is precisely where the major difficulty lies in bringing up teenage children; this is the parents' cross: "the freer the child, the better the job the parents have done, the greater their joy, the fuller their satisfaction. But, at the same time, the freer the child, the more independent he is, the more he belongs to himself, the less he belongs to his parents, the less he is in their hands. What is to be done with this new source of freedom? What will become of the child who is now his own master? What will 'our' child do with his freedom, our child who will always be ours, all the more so for our having loved him so much, but all the more independent and self-sufficient because we have brought him up properly? Nothing can discharge a parent from having to carry this cross in life. He has to walk with it and try to bear it with dignity and intelligence. That is what parenthood means" (Yela, 76).

To sum up: today it is more urgent and more essential than ever before to understand and help the teenager, by looking ahead to the crisis before it descends upon him and trying to protect him from the damaging influences of his environment; but the parents' task of understanding and helping is by no means a straightforward one.

It seems to me that one of the best ways of supporting parents and others concerned with children is to outline certain problems and situations that frequently arise and cause difficulties in normal adolescence. In each case we shall study the nature and causes of the problem and possible ways of helping the teenager cope with it. The literal meaning of the word "problem", *pro-ballo,* is "to throw towards" and here we intend to present each problem as an improvement to be aimed at. However, these problems will not be understood or solved unless we are first aware of the contexts in which they appear. Therefore we begin by outlining the meaning and significance of adolescence — its purpose and function — and presenting it as a period of immaturity seeking maturity.

I think it will also be useful to try to provide an overall, clear, and sensitive description of adolescence. Although there are many books on the psychology of the adolescent, most of them have the disadvantage of being intended for psychologists and not for people involved in actually bringing up youngsters. When reading it is easy to get lost in detailed descriptions or to get confused by the variety and divergencies of opinion put forward by the various authors. It is true that some writers offer a more accessible and comprehensive view of the subject than others, but they seldom present a systematic picture or even a minimally scientific account of the subject. In our own description, we make a distinction between the features of adolescence at all times and the particular characteristics of the situation today. Our contention is that adolescence has always been essentially the same or similar, but that at each historical period it expresses itself in different forms of behaviour. It is not that teenagers change, but the society in which they live does, and this social change in one way or another affects the manner in which they experience a problem which, in itself, is perennial.

In our study of adolescence as it always has been, we discuss three stages: puberty or early adolescence, middle adolescence and later adolescence or youth. This division is based on an obvious fact, namely the considerable differences between an adolescent of twelve, at the beginning of puberty, and another of twenty-one, at the upper end of what can be considered his youth. Adolescence, then, is a very broad period of development, within which continual and very important changes are going on, and no easy generalizations can be made with any degree of confidence. These continual developments have to be closely watched in practice and the process of upbringing adapted to changing circumstances. Otherwise a well-meaning adult can very quickly find himself "ruled out of court".

In distinguishing and describing these three stages, we are basically following a psychologist of acknowledged prestige, Georges Cruchon. They correspond to three phases of adolescence which are easily observed: the beginning (emergence of one's intimacy or identity, crisis of physical growth and sexual awakening), a phase of inner conflict and negative behaviour towards others, and then a period of consolidation, however relative, of the newly discovered personality. The important point to note is that between the child and the youth the distance is not covered by one great leap but by an intermediate

11

age with its own characteristics. The stages are not independent phenomena or watertight compartments; the development is a continual process. Paraphrasing Débesse on the subject of the stages which he distinguishes in childhood, we could say that they are different chapters of one and the same story. What I propose to do is to point out the characteristics of each significant period in the development. I must also mention, however, that the duration of each stage can vary according to the individual and his particular circumstances.

This is very much a matter of opinion, of course, to some extent. One might question, for instance, whether there are three and only three stages or whether they manifest themselves in all adolescents in precisely the same way. These are points which require further study.

In my description of each stage I have thought it important to distinguish what I call its basic or structural features — that is to say, those common to all adolescents — from those that are not common. This will help parents and other readers to understand the extent and application of the description I give. The potential for reaching maturity and the positive forms of help I mention are grouped in terms of these basic features and continually refer to them.

My decision to rely on one expert has advantages and disadvantages. On the positive side, there is the benefit of having a more coherent view of our subject and thus avoiding the dangers of drawing on too many authors. On the negative side, however, I cannot hope to present an exhaustive analysis of the various psychological viewpoints. I confess that the decision to avoid such a psychological method was quite deliberate, because the purpose of this book is totally different. I feel that parents and others involved with teenagers are less interested in a complete treatise on the psychology of adolescence than in having some useful guidelines on the down-to-earth task of bringing up children. What I hope to achieve is an analysis of the adolescent's situation, to help parents detect the strong points (potential for reaching maturity) and the weak points (obstacles on the road to that maturity) and thus set up possible objectives and activities for improvement (positive forms of help).

The last eight chapters of the book are devoted to a detailed study of certain problems of adolescence. A distinction is made between some frequent problems (rebellion, running away from home and shyness) and problem situations requiring guidance (study, choosing a career, free time, money and work). The three problems we have just mentioned do not always arise, but when they do, they affect the youngster seriously and consequently influence his relationships with others; they are also closely linked with the development of his personality. While the situations mentioned are inevitable in the life of every teenager, the problems — if they occur — arise not so much from his personality as from external circumstances and influences.

I also refer to many other problems, though they are treated in less detail. These problems — insecurity, introversion, confused values, following the crowd, the harmful influence of the environment — are set out in the first seven chapters of the book. Although they undoubtedly merit a detailed study in their own right, this will not be possible here: the whole question of adolescence is so enormous and complex that no single study could possibly hope to cover the whole range of problems involved.

For this reason I propose to deal in a later book with certain other problems which arise during adolescence and which nowadays greatly concern parents and teachers. These — which the reader will readily notice are missing from this book — have to do with sex, drugs, ideologies, violence and religion. The fact that I have not dealt with them in this book does not mean they are less important than those I do deal with.

The subject of friendships during adolescence also merits special study, both because of the ways friends can help a person to mature and because of the problems friendships often pose parents. However, this matter I plan to cover in another book, which I am currently writing.

Part I:
The Meaning of Adolescence

1

What is adolescence?

1. Parents and the teenage crisis   A very common situation, which may serve as an introduction to the whole question of adolescence at family level, is that parents seem surprised and disconcerted by the new and unexpected way in which their teenage children behave. During childhood, they assiduously teach them a whole range of habits (obedience, respect, punctuality, tidiness, how to work, good manners, personal decorum) and this training tends to bear fruit up to about the age of twelve. From then on children may begin to stop "behaving well": they become disobedient, refuse to say what they have been doing outside the home, come back late, often get irritated for no good reason, react in a bad-mannered way when their parents express interest in their problems, neglect their personal appearance, leave their room very untidy and so forth.

When they find themselves in this unexpected situation, many parents feel overwhelmed and demoralized: all the effort they spent in bringing up their children seems wasted; all that good example and good advice has not stopped them from becoming irresponsible hooligans. It is not unusual for parents in these circumstances to wonder where they have failed or to ask themselves who has undone all their good work.

Once their initial amazement has worn off, it is quite common for parents to think that their duty is to start all over again. This sets off a period of trying to correct the child, sometimes involving a renewed intensity in their attempts to help and in the demands they make. Yet the desired results do not materialize. The only effect is that the youngster becomes even more irritable, grows even further apart from them and takes pleasure and pride in his newly acquired bad habits. The problem may reach a point where the parents begin to think that it is no longer a question of upbringing but of "law and order".

It might be useful for parents in this situation to look for some expert advice. Basically, this would consist of being told whether

14

the child's behaviour at a particular moment is normal or abnormal, why it occurs and what they should and should not do before and after the change.

The first thing to emphasize about this kind of situation is that the parents involved — and there are many in this predicament — are surprised by the changes in the child's conduct. They are, or wish to be, unaware that children grow up both "quantitatively" and "qualitatively", so to speak, and that this growth necessarily has repercussions in their behaviour. This is quite normal at particular stages and, far from being reprehensible, actually has a function to fulfil in the development of the individual, to such an extent that the most "absurd" and "weird" behaviour may have a part to play in the process of his personal development. Therefore it is wrong for parents or others to become depressed or dramatic about the problem. It is important for them also to realize that the effects of the good example and of habits acquired in childhood are no less useful simply because they temporarily disappear from view. Once the period of those inevitable physical and psychological changes, which are perfectly normal in adolescence, has passed, once the youngster recovers his balance and is calmer, they invariably find that his conduct will become coherent again, but with the difference that now it is much more consciously so than it was in childhood.*

Parents who wonder what mistake they have made in the child's earlier upbringing may put it down to a lack of foresight. The fact is that children grow up without their parents realizing it and time passes very quickly. However, it must be remembered that the term "educate" implies "arriving before" the pupil. We educate for the future as well as for the present.** As adolescence approaches, parents should try to ensure that their children rationally and gradually assimilate the principles necessary, not only for their present, but also for their future conduct. In this way, when the crisis comes,

*This explanation does not preclude the fact that many teenage problems may, in fact, become complicated and fail to resolve themselves satisfactorily for various reasons, internal and external; psychological develpment is certainly less predictable and definite than biological development. Some teenagers also reach maturity without experiencing scarcely any problems along the way.

**Foresight of the kind required of parents is not the same as prophecy. Obviously they cannot be expected to foresee the unknown accurately. What is involved is a type of upbringing which keeps in mind its possible consequences for the future, realizing, for instance, that something a child accepts passively today he may compare favourably with ideas and experiences of his own tomorrow.

the children will have a firm basis on which to rely within themselves while the parents will have a reference point on which to continue the children's upbringing. The principles involved must relate to teaching them about freedom, about faith and about love. Obviously one cannot claim that this will prevent the crisis itself, but the object is that, when it does come, it should be as mild as possible and parents and children should have previously established some kind of intercommunication to make it easier to deal with the new problems.

So we are not concerned here with "starting from scratch" or with "beginning again", in the sense of going back over the childish principles and repairing the damage done; I am suggesting that the individual should be treated as he or she is at this moment: an adolescent, a teenager, not a child. The new situation demands that we set new objectives. Sometimes this attempt to "begin again" derives, not so much from some flaw in our knowledge of the youngster, but rather from a desire or wish to prolong the relationship of dependence which existed during childhood, either through resistence to change or fear of the future. This attitude is undoubtedly the main obstacle to understanding and getting on well with teenagers; it is a parent's gravest mistake at this stage of their development. The important thing is to stimulate and encourage their sense of autonomy, far from repressing it, but without confusing it with a mere desire for independence or freedom from all restraint.

If we fail to acquire an adequate understanding of the teenage phenomenon — its causes, manifestations and significance — it will be very easy to make the mistake of making moral judgements on actions and reactions which, at least in principle, are in no sense either "good" or "bad", and this makes it difficult to develop a correct conscience in the teenager. If an imaginary bad intention is imputed to his behaviour ("He just does it to annoy me"), we run the risk of transforming his upbringing and education, the process of improving him, into a mere question of our own pride.

2. The discovery of one's self   The significance of adolescence can be treated in a meticulous analytical, descriptive manner, as is sometimes done in academic books on the subject. However, I feel that this approach is of little use to parents. Instead of an exhaustive description of its psychological features, what parents need is an overview, a comprehensive picture of the phenomenon. Adolescence is, above all else, a time of special growth which goes from childhood to adulthood: the adolescent is someone who is growing, as distinct from the adult, who has already grown. Throughout the period of childhood there has been a process of uninterrupted growth, but this becomes much more significant and rapid as the child approaches the age of twelve.

Growth is both quantitative and qualitative. We witness not only an increase in size and weight, in mental capacity and physical strength, but also a transformation in the child's own self, in his personality.

Adolescence marks the beginning of a qualitative growth, in other words, the birth of something in the person: not the birth of the person, but of something in him or her, and that something is precisely his own intimacy or personality.[6]

The emergence of a person's intimacy comes about, slowly and laboriously, throughout the early teenage years. At first, there is simply a feeling of his own self: he feels that he has something within him that belongs to nobody else, something very much his own. This is an emotion that surprises and even discourages him for a time, giving him a surreptitious kind of satisfaction and unease. Later on, this feeling, this impression, becomes something more conscious and reflective, namely the actual discovery of his own self. The consciousness of a child, closely associated with the collective, is replaced hesitantly but steadily by a more personal consciousness. When this happens, the child's world crumbles; there is a break with the past; and with the attitudes of grown-ups.

The discovery of himself, of his own ego, allows the teenager to become aware for the first time of a number of personal possibilities which were previously unknown to him. This in turn allows another tendency to develop which, as a requirement inherent in life, is in a way common to all living things, namely the affirmation of one's self, of one's personality: self-assertion.

One of the most valuable sources of information on these questions is provided by diaries. In one diary,[7] a girl of sixteen says of a book she has been reading: "I hate reading books of this type because they tell me things I should find out for myself. That's why I never read this kind of stuff". On another page she refers to a friend who wants to go to Switzerland to work "at anything she can get" and writes: "She wants to go just to prove to herself that she can cope, that she doesn't need them" — that is, her parents. Self-assertion is a feature that runs through the teenager's whole development; it means wanting to be able to cope on one's own; the youngster wants to — and indeed ought to — learn to get along by himself, without needing parents or teachers to act as buffers, as they did when he was a child. Many traits of teenage behaviour are nothing but an outward expression of this inner assertion: obstinacy, the desire for total independence, a tendency to contradict all the time, especially to contradict parents at every opportunity, a desire to be admired, a wish to break away from home and to rebel against all rules. This tendency towards self-assertion, in itself normal and necessary for the development of the personality which is just emerging, can become quite extreme if met with negative attitudes on the part of grown-ups, if they are over-rigid, if they lack understanding or are arbitrary in their exercise of authority. Yet it often happens that teenagers who are well understood by their parents still claim to be misunderstood: this is their particular way of asserting themselves.

A certain comparison may be drawn between the behaviour at this stage and that of children going from the first to the second phase of childhood, at the age of three approximately. When the parents try to dress or feed them, they object and insist on doing it themselves. Such reactions show a need and a desire to get along on their own, to exercise the abilities just being developed.

3. Development of the self-assertive tendency The tendency towards self-assertion evolves according to age.[8] In the early years (eleven to thirteen in girls, twelve to fourteen in boys), youngsters have as yet no awareness of what is happening inside them and they are oblivious to many of the opportunities which lie within their grasp. There is a second period (thirteen to sixteen in girls, fourteen to seventeen in boys) when they are fully aware of their abilities; their physical strength becomes evident in sports and other contests; they take advantage of every type of situation to test and prove themselves, perhaps even deliberately looking for danger; they express their aggressiveness continually and in every way, ranging from pillow-fights at bed-time to lashing out when they happen to pass a companion. At the third stage, (sixteen to twenty-one for girls, seventeen to twenty-two for boys), there is usually a more positive type of self-assertion. With a greater sense of security in the area of thought and reflection, they are less upset emotionally by things which would have irritated them previously; their conduct is more stable and objective and they are less vulnerable to external difficulties. They achieve a greater degree of self-control and have a feeling of having found their own equilibrium and come to terms with the world around them.

The amount of ground covered in this gradual adaptation to oneself and others is reflected in two items recorded at different times by the young girl quoted above:[9] "I want to get out. I am suffocating here. . . . I must get away. I want to find myself once and for all and that's impossible here." "We also spoke [a reference to a friend] about finding ourselves. We agreed that we find ourselves in our dealings with others, by observing how they behave and why they react to situations in one way or another. I'll make a kind of examination of conscience each night of whatever I have done during the day and I'll ask myself why I have said or done this or that. But in any case, we never totally find ourselves."

The first entry shows how the girl wants to escape from her usual environment, especially the home, in order to find herself, in the belief that this is a hindrance to that objective. Her remarks also denote some emotional instability, with a degree of aggressiveness. On the other hand, in the second entry she no longer seeks herself through flight or escape, but precisely in a personal relationship with others, together with some reflection on her own behaviour. There is also an intellectual process and a personal conclusion: "We never totally find ourselves"; this reflection is quite revealing, in that it shows a step from a dogmatic and idealistic attitude to a more objective and realistic one.

4. Self-assertion, insecurity and growing-up As well as an awareness of one's own abilities and a consequent tendency towards self-assertion, the discovery of one's self produces in the adolescent, from the beginning, "a disturbance of one's sense of security and, consequently, the emergence of feelings of doubt and inferiority".[10] These feelings develop according as external obstacles present themselves and the teenager gets to know his own limitations. There is thus a constant association of self-assertion and insecurity in his conduct. Independently of the influence which unstable feelings may undoubtedly exercise, this association in itself explains the typical alternating movement between states of euphoria or self-complacency on the one hand and periods of depression on the other.

The gradual development of a more objective type of confidence in one's own abilities is necessarily related to greater personal experience; this explains the progress from the immature outlook of early adolescence to the more mature attitudes characteristic of later stages: from obstinate, aggressive self-assertion to a more positive type of assertion of oneself, and from a notion of freedom reduced to mere desire for independence to a concept of freedom as autonomy coupled with service of others.[11]

The teenage drama is derived from the fact that the enterprise of getting ahead through one's own abilities, adapting to one's new role in life, involves a considerable imbalance between the goal to be achieved and the means available to attain it. The teenager's situation is therefore comparable to that of a swimmer between two points (childhood and adulthood), who has very little swimming skill (little practice or experience of life), in waters full of dangers and difficulties (the harmful influence of the environment), who does not know exactly where he is or what awaits him at the other side (disorientation). Yet, in spite of inevitable moments of downheartedness when he feels tempted to give up, the swimmer, for better or worse, continues on his course and manages to reach his destination. How do we explain this surprising feat? Undoubtedly, it is due to the existence in every adolescent of a powerful inner impulse to reach maturity, in other words, to grow up.

The comparison with the swimmer shows how the two attitudes, self-assertion and insecurity, manifest themselves as they play a part in the process of growing up. Self-assertion is the motivating force which initiates the process and keeps it going; insecurity in the face of difficulties and even failures is a critical state which helps the teenager to learn humility and realism, forcing him, on another level, to react positively to failures and adapt to them. All mistakes can at first have a paralyzing and demoralizing effect, but in the long run they provide an incomparable source of personal experience and apprenticeship, showing how useful it may be to call on outside help on certain occasions. Thus the impulse towards maturity, far from dwindling when failures occur, gains strength precisely in such circumstances.

Self-assertion and insecurity are by no means as opposed to one another as might at first appear. In this regard it may be worth mentioning that youngsters can feel insecure precisely because of having attempted too much or gone too far in asserting their own capabilities. It should also be said that they assert themselves precisely when they are most aware of the insecurity of their situation. The two known ways of reacting to insecurity, namely withdrawal and defiance, have one and the same objective, which is to assert or reaffirm the feeling of one's self and avoid any devaluation of one's identity.

This clarification of the significance and function of insecurity in teenagers may open the eyes of parents and others who have to decide what attitude they should adopt, in principle, towards an insecure child. One reaction which they should certainly avoid is an attempt to eliminate the factors that actually cause the insecurity and to take the youngster's place in solving his problems or difficulties. Any unnecessary help is a constraint for the teenager. Such a reaction only deepens his sense of insecurity, hinders him in learning to face the problems of life and stops him from learning through experience. Normally this reaction is rejected by children.

Another equally counterproductive attitude is to be found at the opposite extreme, namely leaving the child to his own devices, without proper help, in the hope that he will resolve his problems by himself. This is tantamount to neglecting the child; it may deepen his insecurity and offer him no satisfaction whatever; in particular, it will create emotional problems. The middle and most positive course is to help him, but only in so far as may be necessary, helping in a way that does not attempt to replace him, but rather guides him, informs him and directs him, while respecting his personal freedom.

Sometimes parents have to face the very real problem of finding a way to arouse in the child a need to be helped if appropriate, even when he does not wish to be helped. Equally it may be difficult actually to refuse unnecessary help when he requests it, without giving the false impression of neglecting him.

Up to now I have dealt with the basic aspects of the adolescent phenomenon. I have only introduced the subject of how and why the phenomenon arises and by no means have I given a full account of it in a way that would allow anyone to get to grips with individual cases. At this point I must emphasise that, in a sense, there is no such thing as adolescence: there are only adolescents. While there are certain common factors, there are many differences between individuals, based on their sex, age, personality and all kinds of environmental influences. Hence, on the subject of education and upbringing, there is no single method that will be valid for all types of adolescent. We might indeed enter into some general considerations of each of the "common" factors, but we must always remember that every child is a "personal and non-transferable" human being and that the situation and circumstances in which he finds himself can be properly known only to someone who lives in close proximity to him.

2

The search for maturity

1. Adolescence: immaturity in search of maturity We have described adolescence as a period of special growth which allows childhood to advance into adulthood. An adolescent — the word comes from the Latin *adolescere* — is one who grows, develops, matures: "Those years still clearly show the sign of movement towards an end, the seal of development, of growth, of maturing" (Wallenstein).[12]

For entry into the adult world, a number of changes are required, steps in the growing up process at all levels, leading to attitudes and behaviour characteristic of maturity. The extent of the changes involved can be seen if we compare a child of twelve or thirteen with a young person of twenty or twenty-one: the former is still obviously childish, he relies for virtually everything on his parents, accepts their responses, constantly seeks their help and protection, while the latter needs to think, decide and act on his own initiative and is in a much better position to face the problems of life. This radical change comes about in a short space of time and shows that the real significance of adolescence consists in the development of personal autonomy. In the midst of his confusion and all his conflicts, the teenager pursues three closely related objectives, namely the attainment of maturity in the sense of a responsible personality, the achievement of independence, so as to think, make decisions and act on his own initiative, and the fulfilment of his own self, so as to be someone in his own right, with a personal and independent existence: in a word, so as to be a person.[13]

Adolescence is therefore to be understood as a complex process of personal maturing, a period of immaturity in search of that maturity which is part of adulthood. The teenager's immaturity is different from that of a child or an immature adult. The immaturity of the child is that of a person who cannot get along on his own but nevertheless does not see that as a problem. The child accepts his dependence on adults in a natural way because as yet he is not conscious of any personal self and therefore has no wish and no need to think or act on his own responsibility or to trust his own judgment. The immaturity of the adolescent, on the other hand, is that of someone who cannot manage on his own but nevertheless feels a desire, an inner need, to do so; and when he tries to cope with things unaided he sets in motion abilities not yet tried out, in other words, immature skills. The adolescent takes risks and has difficulties in dealing with grown-ups; he feels insecure and often fails, because in a very short space of time he has considerably increased the level of his own aspirations in life. If an adult is immature, it is normally due, not to any lack of ability or experience in dealing with new situations, but to lack of effort and an unwillingness to make demands on himself to live according to worthy principles.

If we compare the teenager's attitudes and behaviour with those of the "good child" or the "responsible adult", we may at first think that he has "gone backwards". He is manifestly less tidy, orderly, persevering, conscientious, respectful, sociable, docile or well-mannered than before: but does this mean that he is necessarily less mature or responsible? Clearly not, for now, in spite of these worse "outward signs", he is acting with a higher degree of autonomy. His previous good conduct was largely the result of habits learned by imitating others and passively doing "what he was told". Now, on the other hand, he wants and needs to do things out of personal conviction, and this involves taking a new look at all his previous behaviour. He is in a different and more difficult "ball game", and this shows itself in poorer results. But this should not deceive us it is not usually a retrograde step but a sign of growth and maturity which is normal in adolescence.*

It would be wrong, therefore, to imagine that maturity arrives suddenly at the end of adolescence, while the previous years have been totally immature. From about the age of twelve onwards, there is an "apprenticeship" to facing reality in a personal way. Through the whole process, the boy or girl acts immaturely, but some of this behaviour is essential for the development of the personality, because this develops not only through success, positive results and steps forward, but also through mistakes, failures and steps backwards; very often a step forward would be impossible first having taken several steps backwards or sideways. The teenager matures as he decides to retrace his steps along the road discovered on his own initiative: it is a slow and risky process, but very effective. "The

*This general tendency to act from personal conviction does not materialize in every single case, for some teenagers cease to imitate their parents only to copy others unthinkingly or simply to follow some fashion.

concept of maturity in the adolescent must not be considered as a fixed state or the final point in a development process. Maturity is a relative term, denoting the degree to which, at any juncture in life, a person has discovered and is capable of utilizing the resources to which he has gained access in the process of growing up" (Jersild, 361).

Each stage of development, then, has its own appropriate maturity; the teenager's is not the same as the child's or the adult's. Hence we must examine the maturity proper to the teenager, having first clarified the concept of maturity in general.

A brief look at the learning process, the "apprenticeship", itself, will confirm these remarks. Many writers define an apprenticeship as an alteration in one's behaviour, produced as a result of experience. Precisely for this reason they consider that something is learned every time a person has to face some new situation or resolve some new problem. When confronted with such a problem or situation, the individual looks for some new technique to take successful action. If experience is essential for any apprenticeship, all the more reason to call on experience when, as in the case of the teenager, the problem to be resolved concerns the direction of his whole life. Here the principle is more valid than anywhere else that no one can do someone else's learning for him, because after all the only way to learn to live is by living!

We have seen that immature behaviour can have a part to play in the development of the personality; but even the early adolescent's behaviour can also show certain signs of maturity. Normally at every level of development there is a mixture of the mature and the immature, for two main reasons; first of all, it is commonly admitted that in growth, whether physical or mental, no one ever advances equally on all fronts at the same time and, second, because a sign of immaturity is recognised only after some type of progress has been observed. For example, a very clear feature of maturity which is normally observed at about the age of fourteen or fifteen is the ability to reflect, to go back over one's thoughts about oneself. Yet closely related to this step forward we find an element of subjectivism which views reality entirely through the filter of one's own personal needs and emotions. Such a subjective outlook on things causes the teenager to defend his own opinions at all costs and leads him to such extremism in his judgments that it often borders on outright fanaticism. Obviously this unrealistic attitude will show up only in the light of a new outlook and equally obviously the new realism will be achieved only as a result of a few clashes with reality.

When I argue that the adolescent himself must take the lead throughout the maturing process and when I defend the idea that typical teenage behaviour and features have a function to fulfil, this does not imply that I wish to adopt a permissive stance on the question of upbringing. I am simply suggesting that at this particular stage the individual advances as a result of demands he makes on himself, his "self-upbringing" so to speak, rather than merely by acquiring behavioural habits. Guidance should primarily take the form of encouraging the youngster to be consistent in pursuing noble ideals and carrying out the personal decisions he has freely made. Since adolescence is a period of immaturity out of which normally — though not invariably — one gradually moves, perhaps, before we go any further, we should ask what we mean by maturity, how it is attained and what kind of immaturity provides the starting point. Let us take a look at these points now.

2. What is maturity? Maturity is the result of purposeful, intentional improvement or advancement of the various faculties specific to human beings. It is the result of a process which is not confined to adolescence but, on the contrary, goes throughout the whole of life. In this sense we may speak of physical, intellectual, emotional and social maturity.

A distinction is made by L. Prohaska between maturity and development. Development has to do with the evolution of the person's natural dispositions according to the laws governing physical and mental growth; this has very definite limits for each individual, beyond which no amount of teaching or learning can bring him. On the other hand, "the potential for maturity on the part of any individual goes far beyond these limits, by virtue of a factor that makes the person something more than a centre of subjectivity. In the essence of the person there exists something more than an ego; a second person, 'you', also forms part of it, and not only as a point of reference but as a constituent of one's own being . . . . The person is more than himself. The limits of his maturity extend in so far as he can make that 'extra' his own" (L. Prohaska).[14] According to this concept of maturity, the educational process consists of an invitation to personal effort in order to "excel oneself" inwardly. Such an effort to go beyond oneself produces greater maturity, which Prohaska interprets as directing one's life in accordance with the sense or direction of one's own existence.

Maturity can also be understood as the result of discovering and developing "values": these are "specifications of the good, that is, an entity or being in so far as we perceive it and desire it from the point of view of its perfection. Values are the perfective element of each entity, that inherent quality in the subject which launches it into a movement of perfection, to exceed its limitations, which makes it a being capable of growth. . . . Values are the impelling tendencies which incite man constantly to go beyond his limits" (M. J. Cantista).[15]

Every value is both imminent and transcendent. "It is imminent in so far as it is rooted within man's being: it is a quality of his nature; it is transcendent in so far as man is never complete but continually tends towards something beyond himself, which finds its completion only in the personal being of God, the absolute value" (Cantista).[16] Since personal improvement consists of growth, then, all education and all upbringing consists of instilling values into the learner. A distinction may be made in this regard between values by which the human being is defined as a person and others by which that person fulfils himself. Among the former we find, for instance, individuality or singularity, intimacy, fidelity and autonomy.

Individuality, singularity, "selfhood" is the quality of "being oneself," being a person. Its opposite is collectivisation, but not socialisation; therefore it is not just isolation or mere independence. *Intimacy* may be defined as the inner space which I achieve in order to be with myself and which allows me to find myself. It is equivalent to *awareness* of my own individuality. *Fidelity* is to persevere in the logical consequences of one's own convictions and beliefs. *Autonomy* is a value by virtue of which the person becomes the generator of his own actions. "The highest expression of autonomy is the capacity to govern oneself, the capacity to be one's own law, the effective use and possession of one's freedom" (V. García Hoz).[17]

Among the values which allow one to fulfil oneself as a person are moral and religious values.

In the maturity process, understood as the assimilation of values, "the object is to distinguish oneself from others as one's own self; to locate oneself as a person in freedom and responsibility; to forge one's own opinions about the world and one's place in it; to become 'oneself' in order to advance towards others and call them 'you', realizing that one is 'I' (R. Guardini).[18]

This concept of maturity as the capacity to act on one's own judgment and personal responsibility implies that "the essence of maturity consists of a disciplined and responsible personality which will change the adolescent into an adult and equip him to take decisions, to face problems and solve them and to establish relationships with others in a satisfactory manner" (Schneiders, 58). To grasp the meaning of maturity more fully, it may be useful to emphasise the following points, among others:

Signs of intellectual maturity are: independence and objectivity in one's judgment, a critical sense and the ability to adapt to new situations. Expressions of emotional maturity are: self-control in emotional matters, the ability to face problems serenely, acceptance of failure, the ability to reply with moderation and after due consideration, being able to give and take. Signs of social maturity are: tolerance of others, being answerable to them for one's own actions, and willingness to collaborate in collective endeavours.

These three factors are reflected in a definition of maturity as: prudence or sound judgment with which a person governs himself.

We might sum up this whole point by saying that maturity is the result of using one's freedom to develop one's capacities and overcome personal limitations. Self-control — mastery of oneself — and a spirit of service of others are essential in the development of these capacities. Indeed, self-control and service are closely related, in that control of oneself should be directed towards the service of others. Maturity, therefore, is grounded on progress in the attainment of freedom. One matures as one acquires an acceptable level of freedom. This, in turn, implies learning to practise the human virtues.

3. Immaturity, the adolescent's starting-point It may be useful for the teenager to compare his goal (maturity) with the point from which he starts out. This will give him a much clearer idea of the distance to be covered and the type of journey that has to be made.

We have seen that the maturity to be sought consists basically of advancing "beyond" oneself, acquiring a number of permanent values and developing freedom with responsibility. We might ask, therefore, how far the teenager is from these goals when he sets out to achieve them. Without wishing to generalize, for I know that each individual is different, I feel it would be useful nevertheless to look at those features characteristic of immaturity which tend to be common to all individuals, even if they take slightly different forms in each case.

Let us start by looking at some features closely related to the teenager's way of having and exercising his freedom. It is well known that from the beginning of adolescence, boys and girls jealously defend their freedom, to such an extent that it is often the subject that creates most difficulties in their relationships with their parents. Here is an example: "Parents are obsessed with forcing us to live our life as they think best, and they have no right to do this. We are free, free to do whatever we like. They only have a right to warn us, advise us, explain the good and the bad things that may happen, but they should leave us free. They can forbid us to do things only when we are small, when we don't understand, that's all . . . ."[19]

It is quite clear from these remarks that when teenagers ask for freedom, what they often want is nothing short of complete independence. Rules of conduct, they reject as taboos. According to this notion parents and teachers should be limited to giving advice and making suggestions, but should never insist, forbid, correct or punish. Freedom in this sense, then, is reduced to sheer independence but, in principle at least, it is not the kind of independence that consists of thinking, deciding and acting on one'e own initiative (this would undoubtedly be progress); instead it is a matter of rejecting all outside influences: it is a kind of independence which is nothing more than the rejection of dependence on adults. "In the child, the authority of parents and teachers is completely intact . . . . In the case of the maturing person, the psychological situation is essentially different: he feels inclined, by a certain blind impulse, not to acknowledge that any 'outsider' has the right to meddle in his world" (Wallenstein, 213).

The adolescent thinks of freedom quite simply as the absence of external constraints or influences. Therefore even in the most permissive situations he will insist that he is not free; he does not yet realise that freedom, any freedom, is restricted by conditions. Neither does he realise that the main limitations on his freedom are his own personal, inner deficiencies: ignorance, laziness, lack of initiative, selfishness, inconstancy, pessimism etc. When to these limitations we add emotional instability, a sense of insecurity and lack of will-power, it is easy to see that what he lacks is self-control, which is of fundamental importance for the development of personal freedom.

It is also relevant to ask how the teenager understands and exercises that other basic element of his freedom, namely responsibility. Following what we have already said, clearly he is more inclined to be answerable for his actions to himself than to others. He finds it very difficult to take decisions and even more difficult to accept their consequences. Besides, he is much more interested in his rights than in any duties and is only too ready to blame others for his own mistakes.

Closely related to this immaturity in exercising freedom, we find an undeveloped will. In early adolescence, this will is purely "functional", having no clearly defined objectives. At the age of puberty the child does not act out of rational motives, but wants something "because he wants it"; the will is exercised purely for its own sake.

Alongside the development of the capacity for reasoning and critical thought, at the beginning of adolescence a number of structural characteristics emerge which denote intellectual immaturity, such as extremism in making judgments (to which we have already referred) and inability to see shades between black and white, between all and nothing.

These radical attitudes are a consequence both of inexperience in practical life and of the emotional stress that tends to accompany every action. Another symptom of immaturity which is not common to all adolescents has to do, on the one hand, with ability to develop social relationships and, on the other, with the way in which the individual expresses his individuality. Some youngsters in principle avoid social contact with grown-ups because it gives them a feeling of insecurity, and they take refuge either in isolation or in a "gang" formed by their peers; the relationship in gangs of this kind is simply one of comradeship: genuine friendship comes later. Within such small groups, the individual personality is subordinated to the interests of the group and frequently one finds what we would call "following the crowd".

4. Advancing towards maturity   Having defined the goal to be attained, namely maturity, and the starting point, immaturity, we must now say something about the steps to be taken if the goal is to be reached. For this is not something that "happens to one" unexpectedly or by accident. On the contrary, it involves a personal, gradual and difficult struggle, which each individual has to attempt for himself.

The essential task is undoubtedly to establish a system of permanent values and make them part of one's own conduct. These values "are based on their own intrinsic validity and not on fidelity to any particular person, fashion or trend of person" (Carrasco).[20] Plato considered that man is a being between God and the animal, called to advance towards perfection, which is possible only "when he perceives the human possibilities that lead in the direction of the good".[21] The development of this potential Prohaska tells us, involves directing one's life in accordance with the meaning of one's existence.

Naturally this requires perseverance in self-discipline and effort: effort in the discovery and assimilation of values (so as to transform them into motives for the will) and self-discipline so that in practice they may govern one's conduct, as we have already suggested. The effort required to approach perfection depends, ultimately, on love: "Man realises within himself that he is not complete, that he needs to be eternally completed.... When man is seen as the centre, maturity is only maturity of knowledge, but when he is regarded in his existential relation with himself, with his fellow-men and with God, then maturity can be attained as maturity in love" (Prohaska, 60).

On the basis of a scale of allowing him to interpret events and give some meaning and direction to his life, the teenager will be able to fulfil a number of interrelated tasks in order to advance in maturity. These involve a certain learning process aimed at effectively developing freedom with responsibility.

First of all, he must learn to accept responsibilities. For this, he needs to understand that responsibility does not mean simply being answerable to oneself. It also means being answerable, responding, to the calls of others . . . . It implies having to render an account of one's actions and not merely being willing to take the consequences.[22] Then he must learn to accept the outcome both of his own decisions and of those that come to him from others. This, in turn, implies learning to take personal decisions and being responsible for them.

There are three types of decisions, according to the degree of autonomy enjoyed by each individual: those made without having to inform anyone else, those about which others (for instance, parents) have to be informed and those taken after actual consultation with others.[23] In this regard youngsters should have sufficient discernment to know which type of decision is involved in any particular case. To learn to take decisions, it is important to have a fairly clear and objective understanding of any problem and to be aware of the consequences of each possible line of action. It is also essential to have frequent opportunities to take decisions. Normally there is little need to provoke or invent such opportunities, but only to take advantage of those that come along.

Intimately related with decision-making and the acceptance of responsibility is the question of learning to face reality. This is a fundamental goal during adolescence, given the exaggeratedly idealistic outlook on life that teenagers tend to have. Realism is achieved as the individual comes to see things as they really are, rather than as he wishes they were. This involves both learning to see and think more objectively and increasing one's experience of life. Being realistic also requires an objective and realistic view of one's own personal position and the adolescent has to learn to see himself as he truly is, with his potential and his limitations. Such understanding will surely be followed by an acceptance of himself: "I must want to be the person I am, I must want to be really myself and only myself. I must get inside myself, exactly as that self is, accepting the task that is thus entrusted to me in the world . . . . This is the alpha and the omega of all wisdom: to renounce pride, to be faithful to reality . . . . We must be critical of ourselves but loyal to everything that God has placed in us"(Guardini, 22). This advice is valid for any age, but it is particularly relevant at the stage of discovering one's inner self. Accepting oneself is essential if one is to advance along the road of personal development.

Finally, we must mention the importance of learning to live with, and among, others. This implies being able to establish and maintain healthy relationships with them. "The attainment of maturity means the adolescent must learn to combine his newly acquired and still developing independence with a continuing dependence on parents, brothers and sisters. No momentary disagreement or anger should be allowed to destroy the bonds of love. A mature person is one who loves others and acknowledges his dependence on them, while at the same time proudly defending his personal individuality and independence"(Schneiders, 69).

5. Phases in the search for maturity At the beginning of this chapter, we mentioned the considerable difference between an adolescent of twelve or thirteen and one of twenty or twenty-one; the former is still a child, whereas the latter is practically an adult. This clearly shows how mistaken it would be to over-simplify and try to study the whole of adolescence without differentiating between its various phases or ages.

Here we shall distinguish three phases or periods in the process of growing up: puberty or early adolescence, which goes from eleven to thirteen in girls and from twelve to fourteen in boys; middle adolescence, going from thirteen to sixteen in girls and fourteen to sixteen in boys; later adolescence, that is sixteen to twenty in girls and seventeen to twenty-one in boys. These age ranges may vary in individual cases, of course, but they are approximately correct and it must be noted in any case that girls begin and end their adolescence a year earlier than boys.

Puberty is merely an initial phase, marking the transition from childhood to adolescence strictly speaking. At this age the child has not broken completely with his past; we could say that he is a child who is just beginning to leave his childhood behind, so to speak. The process commences with physical and mental development, which have a tremendous repercussion on the child's nervous system: he is astounded and surprised by the changes taking place in his body and whole make-up; he scarcely understands what is going on, what it means, why it is happening or what its purpose is. He is changing but he has no say in the process.

The most significant feature is the development of what we might call his "intimacy", the awakening of the self. This is the first, and most necessary, step in the attainment of an independent personality. The child becomes aware that he is different and distinct from others, and this discovery shakes the self-confidence he unconsciously had during childhood. For the first time, he sees his limitations and his weaknesses and feels alone and defenceless when confronted with them. Hence the first secrets and intimate details begin to emerge. It is a time of emotional and physical instability, a time of great sensitivity (aimed at self-protection), so much so that some experts have called it the "thankless age". Nevertheless, despite this, it is still a period of relative calm.

Middle adolescence sees the final break with childhood and the search for new forms of behaviour. From the mere awakening of the self, a step is taken to the conscious discovery of the self. The individual "gets to know himself, deepens his knowledge of himself, begins to reflect personally, to feel that he is someone and to wish to be more and more so"(Cruchon,61). Self-analysis then becomes the starting point for a rediscovery and a new critical look at the world around him. He no longer confines himself, as in the previous phase, to contemplating simply with amazement the changes he is undergoing or simply reacting instinctively to them, but rather he asks himself questions about them. He wants to know what they mean and he is anxious to adopt a personal stance towards life. While puberty was basically a crisis of a *biological* type with some repercussions on the individual's intellectual development, causing a certain unease ("the unease of puberty" as Débesse calls it), middle adolescence constitutes an *inner* crisis or a crisis of personality. The emotional instability of the previous phase now becomes a downright refusal to conform and a type of aggressiveness. This is "the age of impertinence, a negative phase", because "throughout this period the young person seems to reject everything reasonable and noble, and begins to go backwards" (Wallenstein, 237). These attitudes are doubtless caused by the frustration of not being self-sufficient.

Later adolescence normally sees a recovery of the balance lost in the two previous stages. It is a period of calm, a time to reap the fruit of the seed planted earlier on. The adolescent begins to find and understand himself and he feels more fully integrated into the world in which he lives. Development now slows down and decreases, but it may become more prolonged, especially if there are unfavourable environmental factors. The distinction between the second and third phases is more pronounced than between the first and second. "While the third phase is clearly characterised by the importance attached to moral and spiritual values and by consciously working out a particular concept of life, the second differs from the first rather in the intense repercussions of the physical growth and sexual development on the individual's conduct and attitudes" (Cruchon, 63).

By this time the teenager has passed from a purely negative attitude to a more positive assertion of himself; he is now dominated by a desire to understand and be understood. Hence this phase might be defined as the "awakening of the better self". It is a time for decision-making and a sense of responsibility with a view to one's future, a time for drawing up a plan of life. It is also a time for passionately devoting oneself to noble ideals. "The sublime image of an ideal becomes the great lever for life" (Wallenstein, 253).

Having considered the significance of the three phases or ages of adolescence and the relationship between them, we shall now study each phase in some detail. We will look first at the main features of each phase and then go on to point out some of the positive and negative aspects of the growing-up process. It will end with some possible forms of help for the teenager in the throes of adolescence.

Part II:

The Common Stages of Adolescence

3

Puberty or early adolescence

1. Structural or common characteristics   In puberty, physical development is vitally important because this period is above all a time of anatomical and physiological change, during which the foundations are laid for the child's organism to develop into that of an adult. This development can be seen mainly in physical growth and in the appearance of sexual features, primary and secondary. These features are a sure sign that the child is becoming sexually mature and capable of procreation.

The body begins to grow somewhat abruptly and follows a different pattern for each organ, resulting in a certain disproportion or disharmony: for example, the legs tend to grow quite fast and hence teenagers often seem to be long-legged or "lanky". Any increase in weight tends to result solely from height, because initially there is scarcely any increase in fat. Indeed throughout adolescence phases of growing upwards tend to alternate with phases of growing outwards.

With regard to intellectual development, there is a certain improvement in one's capacity for abstract thought and a tendency to impose some system on one's ideas. Feelings and the imagination exercise particular influence on the workings of the mind and this contributes to changes and inconstancy in interests and opinions. Interests are related not so much to any intellectual curiosity as to sheer eagerness for experience. The intense emotional life characteristic of this phase is more evident outwardly than inwardly. At puberty, the child is a victim of emotional imbalance, reflected in an exaggerated sensitivity and irritability, showing elements of aggressiveness side by side with signs of shyness and tenderness.

A noteworthy feature of the child's emotional situation is the disconnection between the sexual impulse and any feelings of love; physical attraction exists side by side with platonic love without any overlapping between them.

On the social level, the most relevant feature is the tendency to belong to a group of school friends or "mates".

2. Non-structural or particular features   Rapid and unequal growth sometimes gives rise to a certain instability of movement, which may take the form of clumsiness. At puberty, the child feels his new body strange and finds it unwieldy and uncomfortable to live in. He is also rather conscious of his general physical unattractiveness: awkwardness, unpleasant voice, etc. In some cases, the biological crisis may have stronger repercussions than normal in his mental life. This may appear as "being wrapped up in himself", more out of confusion and self-defence than out of any deep thought-process. Thought, in fact, now tends to take the form of day-dreaming, while feelings of insecurity sometimes cause the youngster to take refuge in a purely fictitious world. Such escapism is a defence mechanism and the development of abstract thinking may be affected.

On the emotional level, we notice certain eccentricities, which are both a way of attracting attention and being noticed, and an attempt to dominate in some way the outside world. In some cases also there is a marked tendency to be secretive, to protect one's intimacy and to be cold in one's appreciation of aesthetic matters. On the social level, some children at the age of puberty have particular difficulty in fitting into the world of adults; they feel insecure in that environment and take refuge either in isolation or in a group of friends. Finding themselves in a grey area between childhood and adolescence, they may reject anyone who is a year younger as being "childish", while they find themselves equally rejected by those a year or two older than they are, for exactly the same reason; they are sometimes not invited to parties, for example, by older children.

3. Structural features: positive and negative aspects of growing up   By "positive aspects of growing up" we mean the development of certain abilities and attitudes which, though still in the initial stages, play an important part in the process of advancing towards maturity. By "negative aspects", on the other hand, we mean those inner or outer obstacles that stand in the way of that process. Both the positive and the negative elements derive from the structural features just described.

To take mental life first, the following are positive elements in the growing up process at the age of puberty: consciousness of one's own self, the desire to cope with one's problems, the search for experience, the capacity for abstraction and the development of the imagination. On the other hand, the following are negative elements: unhealthy curiosity and self-sufficiency, manifested as unwillingness to request or accept help. As time goes on, the consciousness of one's self will facilitate the discovery and assimilation of what have been called the values of the person as such, simply by reason of being a human person: his individuality or singularity, his intimacy, autonomy and fidelity. For this to happen, the child has to advance from the feeling or mere awakening of the self to the reflective discovery of the self. This self-knowledge in turn will provide the starting point for a positive acceptance of himself and the discovery of his "better self".

The desire to cope with one's own affairs has a beneficial effect in that it brings into play new capacities, such as the associative memory, the critical sense and the ability to reason. It should also encourage the development of initiative and responsibility. The desire for experience is a positive aspect of that same eagerness which we mentioned earlier; it can be seen both as love of adventure, of excursions and contact with nature and also as an interest in reading and as curiosity of an investigative type: playing with physics and chemistry sets, "inventions" etc. Obviously this particular feature has enormous potential for the child's intellectual education: it motivates the learning process, acquisition of new knowledge, interest in reading and the application of what has been learned. This increase in experience will also lead to a better and broader knowledge of reality, helping the adolescent to be more objective in his judgments. The development of the imagination should reinforce the inventive and creative abilities, so necessary at school and at home.

As far as the emotional life is concerned at this stage, it contributes little to the growing up process, due to the considerable effects of the emotional imbalance to which we have already referred; later on, however, in middle adolescence, some positive elements will emerge. Here, on the contrary, we must mention a negative point, namely the problem of personal relationships or dealings with the youngster, for his irritability, sensitivity and "touchiness" make him almost impossible to live with at times.

On the question of social development, the contact with his peers or companions satisfies his needs at a time when his personality is going through a phase of self-assertion: wanting to be accepted, to have his successes recognized, to communicate with others. These relationships also allow him to swop experiences of all kinds and they provide a good testbed for learning how to get on well with others and develop friendships. However, against this positive element there is a difficulty to be mentioned, namely the danger of slavishly submitting to the peer group. It is often quite remarkable how the same person who rebels against paternal authority can quietly accept dependence on the group and even submit to the tyranny of a group leader. This also shows how the adolescent needs to have demands made on him; without some pressure there will be little progress in the development of personal freedom in any true sense of the word. In this regard, it is beneficial to make demands, provided they are made with understanding and without being unduly authoritative, but continually appealing to the youngster's sense of personal responsibility. Thus, demands imposed by others soon become self-imposed, whereas if they are arbitrary or fail to inspire personal conviction, then they are merely counterproductive.

The negative influence of the environment may further exacerbate some of the problems mentioned. For instance, we might quote some "trendy" opinions that maintain that a person should be answerable for his actions to nobody but his own conscience (irrespective of whether the conscience is properly developed or not), that all authority "alienates" (thus confusing, or trying to confuse, authority in the true sense with authoritarianism or the arbitrary exercise of authority), that a person is "repressed" or frustrated if he adjusts his sexual impulses to the elementary rules of the natural and moral law thus trying to justify any kind of conduct (such as premarital sexual relations in adolescence) in the name of "freedom", which is confused with animal spontaneity. Unfounded opinions of this kind are profusely promulgated by all the media — books, newspapers, radio and television — and are often well received by wide-eyed immature adolescents.

There is currently an attempt being made to educate public opinion to be alert to the undesirable consequences — for people of all kinds — of the mass media when used for advertising purposes, giving information without communication. Such commercial publicity often becomes mere manipulation, which is the "exercise of indirect influence on the human being, in order to encourage consumption (relating to products, sex or new ideas), for the purpose of fostering poor and predictable human behaviour, involving low quality decisions, on the basis of too little reflection and too much emotion" (Otero).[24]

Such manipulation affects adolescents all the more directly (especially at the age of puberty) because they are not protected as adults are. They are particularly susceptible to influence because of certain factors, some of which are common to them all (such as their eagerness for experience) and others of which are not (mental laziness, being favourably disposed to everything new, inability to discriminate in making judgments etc.).

4. Help   In the light of the positive and negative aspects we have just described, we must now ask what forms of help are appropriate for children at the age of puberty. It may be worth stressing at once that any help will be effective only in so far as it encourages the development of individual autonomy and responsibility. There is no point in resolving the youngster's problems for him by saving him the trouble of doing so himself; the best procedure is to direct and guide him, in other words, to give him the information he needs about himself and about the reality he has to face, and then encourage him to act with a sense of responsibility, initiative and effort. Offers of unnecessary help tend to be rejected, because they are usually seen as a desire on the parents' part to prolong the child's dependence on them.

The first type of help ensures that the teenager acquires information about himself and about external reality. This will involve the following:

— Letting him see himself as he really is, explaining what is happening to him and the significance of the changes he is undergoing; getting him to know himself better, with his abilities and limitations. This process, requiring common sense and tact on the part of parents and teachers, should begin before puberty;

— Stimulating his experience of life by taking advantage of his natural desire for such experience; putting him in contact with things hitherto unknown to him, with different points of view on various matters, as well as with different people and environments. This can be achieved by means of a plan for reading involving various types of material: we recommend biographies, accounts of real events and books on nature; excursions and trips to the country or the city and cultural visits to museums, factories, etc. are also very helpful;

— On the basis of his self-knowledge and perception of external reality, it will help to stimulate both acceptance of himself and willingness to request and accept help from others when necessary, for instance regarding methods of study. On this point we should encourage the virtue of optimism, which will involve having confidence in his own abilities and in the help offered by others to face the difficulties that arise.

A second type of help consists of explaining the correct meaning of freedom and its proper use. To achieve this, we should:

— Take every opportunity to get the teenager to think for himself, to analyse facts objectively and learn to identify a problem before taking action, to give careful consideration to all the alternatives before reaching a decision, to practise diagnosing causes and effects in the ordinary events of every day, etc.;

— Explain the meaning and implications of freedom, remembering that many adolescents "confuse anything that limits or lays down conditions with total prohibition, a confusion accompanied by a rather pessimistic — though perfectly human — tendency to think that nothing can ever be done if there are any limitations" (Otero);[25]

— Teach him to see that obedience and acceptance of his parents' guidance are perfectly compatible with personal autonomy: in his choice of friends, the use of his free time, choosing clothes, reading matter, pastimes;

— Give him every opportunity to get used to making personal decisions, encouraging him to give full consideration to the various alternatives open to him and to accept the consequences of whatever decisions he takes;

— Encourage him to develop the virtue of fortitude; it will help to provide him with opportunities to do things through his own efforts and to accept the difficulties that come his way.

A third objective concerns getting on well with others and learning to make good use of free time. On this point we should:

— Encourage the teenager to be flexible in his social relations. This is closely related to respect for others: a type of behaviour which might be appropriate in the presence of certain people might be unsuitable in the presence of others.[26] Respect for others may be exemplified in points such as treating everyone considerately, not gossipping or criticising, and thanking people for favours;

— Teach him to make sensible and constructive use of his free time; this will involve, among other things, suggesting activities which allow him to be busy all the time; it also includes giving him advice on reading matter, on choosing his friends and pastimes (see Chapter 13).

A fourth objective relates to guiding him on how to protect himself from the harmful influence of the environment, especially concerning manipulation in advertising, sexual matters and questions of right and wrong. This will involve "opening his eyes" and providing him with sufficient information, depending on his age, about the dangers of manipulation, its methods and effects. It will also be essential to encourage him to reflect and develop a critical sense, so as not to accept indiscriminately everything suggested or offered to him.

Adolescents also need to develop sound principles on spending money, on questions of sex and on proper values, so that they may learn to resist the whims and needs they create for themselves (with the aid of publicity and advertising) and adopt an attitude of nonconformity, of going against the fashion and saying "no" when necessary. The virtue of moderation will allow them to "distinguish between what is reasonable and what is self-indulgent" and to make reasonable use of their senses, time, money, energies and so on, in accordance with true and upright principles.[27]

4

Middle adolescence

1. Structural or common features   In middle adolescence, the anatomical and physiological growth process which began at puberty continues, but this is no longer the predominating factor. The actual pace of physical growth slows down while the body begins to take on the shape and proportions of an adult. On the intellectual side, the process is seen in a new capacity for abstract thought and a greater power of reflection and critical sense than in the earlier phase.

However, side by side with these factors, which undoubtedly show mental development, we still find something characteristic of earlier stages, namely a certain lack of objectivity. The adolescent's ideas are still strongly affected by an intense emotional life, which often leads to confusion of the ideal with the real and the subjective with the objective. This lack of objectivity explains why a teenager will often defend his opinions in a very dogmatic way.

On the emotional level, the maturing process now shows definite enrichment, due to a deepening of the individual's intimacy. "The adolescent needs to experience in his consciousness and in his emotions everything that adults are capable of giving him and that he, in turn, can give them back. . . . Thus on the level of experience and reflection, his very private inner life and solitude is the forge in which his image of himself is shaped. . . . In discovering his own inner freedom, he learns to respect others' freedom all the more by learning to know himself. . ."(Cruchon, 208).

As he delves more deeply into his own intimacy, the youngster becomes more introverted, and certain attitudes emerge showing strong feelings of self-assertion with regard to his personality: obstinacy, stubbornness and a tendency to contradict. "The youngster closes up and refuses to listen to anyone who tries to convince him by reasoned argument; he obstinately holds on to provocative points of view and imprudent decisions. He resists orders, either openly or passively. Far from attaining the desired effect, any attempt to command him violently or vigorously simply strengthens his obstinacy" (Wallenstein, 239). These personality-asserting attitudes usually tend to involve some degree of aggressiveness.

An important feature of the emotional growing-up process at this stage is the need to love, which forms the basis of friendships and of "first loves".

In the area of social development, a significant feature is the step from mere companionship to genuine friendship. The "gang" or group of companions at the age of puberty was made up of boys or girls of the same age, from the same class at school or living in the same area, who identified with others in a situation similar to their own. The relationship was one of "pals" or comrades, just to do things together and share experiences; as yet there was no genuine exchange of personal views on life. The teenager of fifteen or sixteen is no longer satisfied with this rather superficial relationship, for he is now getting to know his own and others' intimacy. From now on, the "big gang" of playmates tends to be replaced by a group of friends, composed of a chosen few. Within this smaller group, there is much closer communication and feelings, not just of comradeship or companionship, but of deeper friendship. Later on he will feel a need to devote himself more fully to others and establish a deeper, more personal relationship. This will mean replacing the group of friends, in its turn, by just one or two at most. The feeling of being different from others makes him look for a friend who will understand him and with whom he can share his plans, hopes and even failures. It is a typical feature of friendship at this stage that the "best friend" often functions as an idealized *alter ego*, to whom he can attribute all the qualities he would like to find in himself; the "best friend" becomes a kind of model.

Another feature of this phase is shyness; indeed, according to Jean Lacroix the adolescent is shy by nature. This arises from mistrust of himself and others, taking the form of fearing their opinion and attaching exaggerated importance to it. The explanation for this is the difference between the almost unconscious security of the child, who does practically nothing but accept his parents' ideas, and the insecurity of the adolescent, who is no longer fully satisfied by these. When someone rejects ideas received from others, "he will be more likely to doubt and mistrust himself. . . . In fact, shyness is a form of isolation, and one is isolated when one changes environment or when some inner change makes one feel that the environment in which one has been brought up is strange or different" (J. Lacroix).

2. Particular features   Teenagers who were clumsy at the age of puberty now begin to recover control of their limbs, a tendency which may be helped by playing sports. Improvement in the shape and proportions of the body also helps to get rid of any worry about being physically unattractive and, in some cases, this may be replaced by a certain narcissistic attitude.

The development of a critical sense sometimes gives rise to systematic doubt about the intellectual authority of adults; adults begin to lose their mystique, which is transferred to friends, writers, pop stars . . . . Sometimes we also find great enthusiasm for getting at the truth on subjects that arouse the teenager's interest, together with a desire to have "ideas of his own". The development of his intimacy or personality causes in some cases an exaggerated sense of shame or modesty, not so much in relation to his body as with regard to his inner life. Sometimes also the aggressiveness of this phase becomes extreme, giving rise to rebellion and acts that deliberately flout the law and morality.

Some teenagers even begin to boast of this kind of behaviour and seem proud of their defects. How do we explain this attitude? One possible explanation is that "the youngster would dearly like to be important and inspire admiration by his great deeds. But in the present circumstances he finds that as yet he is unable to do anything and no one takes his affairs seriously. He therefore resorts to things that are within his competence: vulgarity, brutality, violence and lawlessness. All of this, however, deep down is nothing but a defence and protection of his own personality" (Wallenstein, 240).

Normally the problem of social integration becomes less troublesome at this stage, but in some cases difficulties do persist. The "best friend" is often the only person to whom some individuals will open up. Others may lapse into total silence, especially within the family or at home; they may spend hours with their parents without uttering a single word. This should not necessarily be interpreted as a symptom of being out of touch with the family; in many cases it is simply that the teenager has nothing to say or is unwilling to say it because of some emotional blockage.

3. Positive and negative aspects of growing up   With regard to mental activity, we may detect as positive aspects at this stage the development of a critical sense and a deepening of objective realistic self-knowledge. On the negative side, there is a tendency to be over-critical, even gratuitously so, and to discriminate nonconformism and rejection of any help whatever from parents.

A person's critical capacity offers genuine potential for the attainment of personal maturity if it is properly developed, that is, if it is a healthy critical sense and not merely "criticism" for its own sake. A critical sense is something found in mature people with intellectual curiosity and an ability to discern. A person with a developed critical sense is not one of the crowd, cannot be easily manipulated and will not become "indiscriminately critical or systematically mistrusting, but a responsible person who forms his own opinions on a sound basis and maintains them" (P. Rodriguez).[29] By indiscriminate criticism is meant criticizing for its own sake, without good cause; it derives from having a shallow basis to one's own ideas, thereby showing no proper examination of the matters in question and little realism. The favourite target for teenage criticism is the behaviour of adults, especially parents. Teenagers often point a scornful finger at any incongruity they find in their parents' lives, their disinterest in cultural matters or their membership of a bourgeois society. They criticize them for being out of touch and insensitive to the youth of today; they accuse them of being behind the times, having old-fashioned ideas and attitudes to education that might have been valid for teenagers of times long past or even for young children today, but not for adolescents. They react particularly strongly against being mistrusted or patronized.

The emotional and social aspects of growing up share the potential, already mentioned, for genuine friendships and service to others. Together with this positive element is the difficulty that "the need to love is still undifferentiated and laden with sentimentalism, even sensuality . . . . Such friendship occasionally has traits of passionate love: obsessional thinking about the other person, a manifest desire to possess without rivals . . ." (Cruchon, 227). Another problem is that parents tend to be relegated to second or third place in favour of friends. The "gang" provides the necessary atmosphere of understanding, acceptance and security for the development of the personality, but it carries the danger of "distancing the young person from his family and school environment, which is a daily reality to which he should adapt. Therefore it must not become a 'hideout' barring the way to life" (Cruchon, 227).

Shyness is also an obstacle to emotional and social maturity, both because it limits and conditions the youngster's activities, reducing the effectiveness of his actions, and because it cuts him off from others (see Chapter 10).

On the question of the harmful influence of the environment, our earlier remarks relating to puberty are still applicable to middle adolescence. Although his critical sense can now be relied on to prevent him from being deceived or lead astray, the fact that he may not tend to speak to his parents about personal matters clearly presents its dangers.

4. Help When thinking of possible ways of helping teenagers, we must take into account a particular difficulty already mentioned, namely their refusal to accept, or even their outright rejection of, any help offered by grown-ups especially parents. The problem is how to help someone who refuses to be helped. Before attempting to answer this question we must look at the motives of fourteen to seventeen year-olds for behaving as they do. Obviously they want to be able to cope on their own. From this point of view, an offer of help from parents will be interpreted as offensive: they feel they are being treated as children. They consider such help unnecessary, either because, in fact, it is so (in the case of over-protective parents) or because their own inexperience makes them feel very self-sufficient. Sometimes, too, although they are aware that they need help, they reject it because they are offended by the way in which it is offered.

This reasoning leads us to suggest that:

1. Help should be offered only when the youngster is aware that he needs it or at least is willing to accept it. Otherwise the rejection will be all the more definite. Therefore the best approach is to try to ensure that the teenager becomes conscious of his own limitations and wants to be helped when he genuinely needs help.

Sometimes the best way of doing this is to let him make a mistake. Nor is there any point in expecting him to ask for help openly: he would probably never do this anyway, because it would be humiliating for him. One has to be able to detect that the situation is appropriate.

2. One has to take great care in the way one offers or provides help. Any method which humiliates the youngster or puts him in an embarrassing position should be avoided. The best thing is to make it look like a joint effort, a collaborative attempt to solve a particular problem. There is no point in making a decision for him or acting instead of him; rather, one should place him in a position to do the job better himself, getting him to think about certain points, giving him hints or bits of information, advising him on how to do the work etc.

By "help" we not only mean guidance and advice on how to do something; we also include all educational methods used by parents and teachers to get youngsters to overcome any difficulties they may find as they advance towards maturity.

Education and guidance at this stage should concentrate basically on two points, namely the individual's character and his relationships with others, especially parents and friends. On the former point, we may notice dogmatism, aggressiveness and shyness, and on the latter, we may find that parents are relegated to second place in favour of a very small number of friends. We must also refer here to the need for guidance on certain specifiic points: study, choice of a career, use of free time, spending money and work. We shall return to these topics in the last part of the book.

On the question of dogmatism in the expression of opinions, advantage may be taken of a strong point in this phase, namely the development of the ability to think logically. An extremist position may often be broken down by asking a number of relevant questions which force the person to think and produce arguments to justify the opinions expressed. This will sometimes show that extreme statements are quite unfounded and full of contradictions or, at least, that there are other valid points of view and alternative ways of considering the matter. Another way of helping youngsters to overcome this defect is to provide them with facts on the subject under discussion or refer them to sources of information which may broaden their viewpoint. Obviously what one should never do is to enter into an argument on their own level in order to defeat their contentions: this only creates an atmosphere of tension in which very often the youngster will exaggerate his position even more in an attempt to protect his threatened ego.

The aggressiveness of this age, expressed in the form of obstinacy, stubbornness, bad manners etc., will not be diminished by violence or inflexibility. In this regard it is vital that parents should not be carried away by their own pride and try to "pay them back" in kind. It should never be forgotten that "the root of these difficulties is not malice, but immaturity, inexperience, inability to cope with a situation. This whole phenomenon is like psychiatric illness . . . . Patience and love, together with gentle firmness, are the means to get the youngster out of his impertinence" (Wallenstein, 245). It is essential on this point that parents should keep calm and be very moderate in their words and actions. Any "drama" from their side will only be counterproductive. When the child is being aggressive it is often best, for instance, simply to ignore his behaviour first of all, pretend not to notice and just wait until he calms down. Then, later, it may be useful to have a chat with him, in a calm atmosphere, trying to get him to analyse his behaviour impartially and draw some conclusions of his own. This will also encourage him to get to know himself and to be strict with himself (see Chapters 8 and 10).

On the subject of being relegated to second place and superseded by a group of friends, parents should be able to resign themselves to this in a "sporty" way, realizing that such behaviour is quite normal at this age and in keeping with the development of the child's personal autonomy. Although this is undoubtedly one of the hardest things for parents to take, it satisfies a need in the child's development to be allowed to break away from them gradually. Naturally we are not suggesting that parents should give up all hope of influencing their children or having a say in their choice of friends. To avoid conflict on this point, they should try to find out about the kind of friends they have and then, in a tactful way, give them whatever advice they think suitable. One way of bridging the gap between the teenager's acquaintances and his membership of a family is that the house should be open to them all from the very beginning. This has the added advantage of allowing the parents to get to know them personally and be able to form some opinion of them.

There is a common denominator in all of these forms of help, namely an understanding firmness or firmness with understanding. Eduard Spranger stresses "the infinite desire to be understood which is felt precisely at this period", but he sees understanding of parents and teachers as a double-edged weapon: "This understanding may debase, if it accentuates the less noble aspects, whereas it may raise up, if it encourages flights on high, proper to the young soul. The only educational method for these years is an understanding that elevates" (Spranger).[30]

We might end this section by stressing that, because at this stage teenagers are deeply influenced by values personified by particular individuals, they should be helped to discover models worthy of imitation. Undoubtedly, good example set by parents is also a decisive factor, especially if related to those virtues which are most essential at this age: self-control, optimism, fortitude and moderation.

5

Later adolescence

1. Basic features   We have already suggested that later adolescence is a period of calm to recover lost equilibrium. Normally it is a time for reaping the fruits of the earlier stages. The young person of sixteen to twenty begins to have an understanding of himself or herself; he is in a better position to take personal decisions and to fit into the world of grown-ups. About this time he also begins to be aware of a certain responsibility in regard to his own future, unlike the child and the early adolescent who think almost exclusively about the present. The young person is now commencing , in his own way, to construct his life.

At this period one could say that, in a sense, there is a new awakening and a new kind of self-assertion, very different from the situation at puberty. His personality has attained a certain level of maturity and by now the individual has some awareness of his own capabilities and limitations. Hence there is an awakening of the "better self", that is, a positive affirmation of oneself. At this point there is a desire to abandon the negative belligerence of the previous phase and an ambition to make progress, closely related with the setting up of an ideal. We must distinguish this ideal of later adolescence from those of earlier phases. The latter are abstract and multiple: justice, equality, liberty, love, truth. . . ., and they lend themselves to an idealistic view of the world. The sixteen to twenty year-old is dominated less by such abstract ideals than by one great ideal conceived as specific and singular.

The awareness of one's responsibility to one's own future, together with the establishment of choice of an ideal, normally encourages the young person to draw up some kind of plan of life — not a detailed blueprint but at least an attempt to give meaning to his life in the future. At this period, physical maturity also reaches its fulness, with a considerable increase in strength and skill, although there is little actual growth in stature because this has practically finished by the end of the middle phase.   With regard to mental development, no new abilities emerge at this stage, for intellectual capacity has defined itself in the previous period. However, there is a certain deepening of thought and an advance from thinking about oneself to reflection on ideas and values: "A type of thinking is ready to come into play which revolves, not so much around oneself, as around the relations between oneself and the world of things and other persons, in the technical, moral, social and religious fields — relationships discovered little by little through study, experience and knowledge. The need to effect a synthesis in this chaos of knowledge, transmitted or learned, and the desire to work out one's own opinions, one's personality and one's judgment on the values of existence reach maturity at the same time as personal positions are adopted" (Cruchon, 337).

At this stage, the young person already posesses practically the intelligence of an adult. He has made progress in coherent, logical thinking and he is in a better position than before to express his opinion with a certain degree of objectivity and realism. There is greater self-control in his thought, which is now freed to a great extent from the distorting influence of emotional imbalance. On the level of emotions, there is an increased interest in members of the opposite sex and a certain ability to "come out of oneself" and establish personal relationships. Though it certainly existed previously, this attraction of the opposite sex was not so highly developed. There is also a certain integration of sex and love or *eros*, of instinct and sentiment, which were rather more separate in earlier stages.

On the social level, significant progress is usually made in overcoming the problem of shyness and social awkwardness. The individual normally develops a wider range of relationships and more acquaintances than previously, while the single friendships tend to disappear. He gets on better and more constructively with his family and has less difficulty in reconciling his own autonomy with a natural and necessary degree of dependence on others. This is possible now, among other reasons, because he has formed a more objective opinion of his parents. Also on the social level, career interests begin to emerge; indeed, this is the time when people usually choose a vocation or career.

2. Non-structural or particular features   On the physical level, some young people take an interest in events and activities that involve a certain risk. A liking for competitive sports also allows them to test their skills and strength. With regard to intellectual maturity, some take a passionate interest in particular cultural activities. On the emotional level, at this stage some have developed quite a high degree of self-control in matters relating to their feelings and emotions. This may be seen, for instance, in the calm way in which they are able to judge their own and others' limitations. As far as social development is concerned, we may mention the ability to integrate positively into the environment of work, whether doing a full-time job or combining a job and study at the same time.

3. Basic features: positive and negative aspects The fact that certain features of later adolescence denote maturity should not be taken to mean that at this stage people are now fully mature. This is something to be aimed at throughout one's entire life but is never fully attained: at best, one achieves a relative degree of maturity. It is worth noting, besides, that the positive aspects to which we refer are simply tendencies, dispositions, which may be developed or stunted at any point. Here, as in the earlier stages, there is potential but there are also difficulties in the process of growing up.

Undoubtedly one of the most positive factors is the desire, already mentioned, to form one's own opinions and judgments on the question of values. This is an essential step in the ongoing development of sound principles and personal judgment. "The development of one's principles and judgment is the touchstone, the acid test, of a true education, because the quality of education can be summed up in the development of free men with principles of their own to be able to judge and decide what they should do, with practical aptitudes and initiative to utilize, and if necessary to change, the world around them" (García Hoz).[31]

Another very positive factor is the desire to improve, to advance beyond their own limits, to educate themselves. It is towards this objective that all education and upbringing acquired previously, both from parents and from teachers is, or at least should be, directed. The typical hyperactivity of youngsters, which allows them to apply and exercise their new-found abilities, is at the service of this positive factor. Finally, we may mention the potential involved in dealing openly and frankly with others, which is a constant source of personal enrichment and experience.

On the negative side, we must refer first of all to a common risk, namely the danger of having personal aspirations which go beyond their abilities. This danger arises from a certain "superior attitude" which often accompanies the considerable advance made towards maturity during this phase. It is usually associated with a passionate ideal, in so far as it gives rise to unrealistic plans for life.

Another difficulty arises from changes in school or starting one's first job. It is often difficult to adapt to these new situations because they may be very different from anything that went before or may require great personal effort, and this effort is demanded just when the youngster has left the problematical middle phase of adolescence and is most in need of a period of rest or consolidation. If this last phase is prolonged more than usual because of continuing studies or circumstances that prevent one starting work, as frequently happens nowadays, there may even be a recurrence of certain problems already resolved: for example, conflict in relationships with parents.

4. Help One way of deciding what forms of help are most necessary in later adolescence is to compare the level of development attained with some basic traits of maturity itself. The following are the traits outlined by Cruchon:

1. More extrovert than introvert
2. Control of emotion
3. Ability to consider others
4. Objective judgment
5. Ability to undertake and fulfil responsibilities
6. Ability to accept failures and rebuild one's life.

A symptom of the predominance of extroversion over introversion is a decrease in day-dreaming and mental escapism, especially after the age of twenty-one. This does not imply that reflection should decrease or that solitude will be systematically avoided. As well as the solitude of the outcast or the pathological escapist, there is another kind, involving a "personal deepening as a preparation for new encounters, to reflect on the problems of life and to rest after the excessive agitation provoked by modern living" (Cruchon, 353).

Among the common features of later adolescence we have mentioned one which is closely connected with extroversion, namely the ability to relate to others in more varied, constructive and extensive ways than previously. Nevertheless, it is usual for youngsters to seek external excitement (especially loud music) and to avoid silence and solitude, which are so necessary for someone to come to terms with himself.

On the level of emotional control, there is some progress over earlier phases; however, the emotions may still exercise too much influence over the reason, sometimes giving rise to volatile behaviour. The ability to consider others is connected with the sentiment of generosity, which is characteristic of later adolescence. It comes from placing oneself in second place and having respect for the freedom of others. However, this attitude is all too frequently exercised only towards members of one's own group, with whom it is relatively easy to get on well, while it is usually quite difficult to accept the demands and requirements of outsiders.

Objectivity of judgment manifests itself in a desire to seek facts to support one's ideas. Youngsters, however, tend to be influenced by their own personal choices and prejudices. Normally one's capacity to assume responsibilities and fulfil them increases during this phase. However, the increase is only beginning to emerge and youngsters are capable of no more than very partial responsibility.

In later adolescence, the young person is far from being able to accept failure and rebuild his life. The will always has its limitations, but at this stage of easy depression these are particularly evident.

In order to make progress towards the six traits of maturity outlined above, the following forms of help may be suggested for adolescents at this stage:

1. Teach them to face reality and avoid all forms of mental escapism. Advise them to learn to protect themselves from external distractions and to seek inner silence;

2. "Help them to accept themselves with all their weaknesses, not to give in to them, but to overcome them patiently by making the best use of their good points" (Cruchon, 355);

3. Teach them to open up to people who think differently from themselves and to spread out from their own little group;

4. Advise them to consider points of view opposed to their own and try to interpret them properly;

5. Teach them to bear the difficulties that come with any responsibility, whether relating to themselves or others;

6. Convince them that "where there's a will there's a way" and they can achieve more than they think if only they are determined to do so.

Part III:

Particular Features of Youth Today

6

Adolescence, a prolonged crisis

Having attempted to analyse the significance of adolescence, as well as some of the positive and negative factors in its different stages, we must now ask a question: Is the teenager of today the same as the teenager of the past and, if he is different, to what extent will the description we have outlined in the preceding chapters help to explain his behaviour?

There are, in fact, some grounds for believing that "adolescence today has ceased to be the beautiful romantic period of our ancestors .... Observations over the last ten or twenty years show that young people today no longer fit, in many ways, the classical model to be found in older works on psychology" (M. J. Hildebrand).[32] Nevertheless, it would seem that today's adolescent is not fundamentally different from his predecessors, even though his external conduct has changed. In fact he is no different from the adolescent of yesterday: it is the world around him that is evolving more rapidly than before and is forcing him to adopt new attitudes, some of which are not altogether healthy: his "depersonalization" or lack of personality comes from today's society.[33] In support of this contention, we might say that "In certain essential aspects, people do not change from one period to another .... Deep down in human nature there are certain constant elements which neither time nor the history of social change can alter .... At any particular moment, the primary basic needs of the adolescent personality are the same", and yet, "in spite of everything, the adolescent of today is different" (Schneiders, 154).

The experience of teachers tells us that each of the two analyses is partially correct. The teenager of today is not radically different in personality from his predecessors, but neither is he exactly the same. We agree with Cruchon that it is mainly society which has changed. However, we must also agree with other writers that social change has had serious repercussions not only in the forms of external conduct but also in the character of today's youth. An example of

53

this, as we shall see throughout this chapter, is that today's teenager is more complicated and poses new problems, especially in his relationships with adults.

The description given in the previous chapters has attempted to outline the characteristics of adolescents without limitation of time, valid in principle for all periods. In a way, however, it was presented from the viewpoint of today: for example, we often referred to the harmful influence of today's environment. We considered that a study of this type was essential before going on to examine the specific problems of the youth of our time, although on its own such a study would be insufficient. In this chapter, therefore, we intend to deal with the features typical of today's adolescent. In our opinion, these are the result of five phenomena that have arisen in the society in which we live: precociousnes in physical development, the emergence of adulthood later than previously, group consciousness among youngsters in opposition to adults, the influence of the mass media and the effects of certain social changes.

1. Precociousness in physical development Some experts maintain that nowadays adolescents are somatically precocious and this manifests itself mainly in earlier sexual maturity. We must also point to the fact that physical growth is earlier and on average tends to be greater than in previous ages. "The physiological changes which govern physical growth and puberty now manifest themselves more precociously than previously, in some countries being almost two years ahead of what was normal fifty years ago, and they appear unexpectedly in individuals who have barely left their infancy behind" (Cruchon, 9). One finds, therefore, "an advance and acceleration in the process of maturation . . . . What would have passed as precociousness thirty or fifty years ago has today become average, and what was previously regarded as average development is seen today as slow progress. Together with the premature sexual processes of maturation, there is also greater physical growth" (Hildebrand).[34]

It must be mentioned that this physical precociousness is not usually paralleled by a corresponding maturity of personality. What are the causes of this imbalance? It is by no means easy to be definite on this point but probably the higher standard of living nowadays (better food, hygiene, medical services etc.) and certain environmental factors (reading, television etc.) play an important part.

Among the consequences of such physical precociousness, we must mention that naturally the puberty phase now lasts longer, in many cases from the age of ten to thirteen in girls and from eleven to fourteen in boys. Another consequence is the premature interruption of childhood: "If sexual maturity now makes its appearance two years earlier than in times gone by, this does not mean, for example, that childhood passes more quickly, but only that its end is cut short" (Hildebrand). This imbalance between somatic and mental maturity may be prejudicial to the harmonious development of the teenager's personality, which is sometimes poorly consolidated as a result. There is also another danger, namely that parents and teachers may be unduly impressed by the child's premature physical growth and mistakenly think that there is bound to be a direct proportion between his physical and psychological development. These teenagers with such an advanced level of vitality but the mental life of a child are often taken to be "older than they really are and this also leads us to expect more from them than they are capable of giving" (Hildebrand).

Obviously problems arise as a result of this partial precociousness of today's adolescents. The cutting short of childhood by the changes involved in earlier puberty may have repercussions later one, because in the growing up process there can be no leap-frogging. To be a healthy, mature, well-balanced adult, one needs to have experienced childhood fully. Another equally important problem, though perhaps more easily resolved, concerns the danger of making excessive demands on the youngster; parents and teachers must realize that in the initial stages they are dealing with a mere child and not yet with an adolescent.

2. Belated adulthood In connection with today's youth in particular, it is clear that "the complexity of social life and staying on later at school or college delay their assimilation into the adult world, in which adolescents in primitive societies and the teenage apprentices of the industrial world not so long ago were launched at an early age. This means that they work out their own system of values between the age of twenty and twenty-five" (Cruchon, 9).

The late development of adulthood together with the earlier onset of puberty means the period of adolescence is considerably longer than previously. The crisis is therefore prolonged and two achievements in particular, which could have been expected between the ages of seventeen and twenty, namely freedom with responsibility and the choice or setting up of an ideal, are now delayed. If, to the long period of training for work, we add the fact that youngsters are usually distanced from their family during that period and in close contact with other members of the peer group, we can see that this is one of the main reasons why today's teenagers occupy a world of their own.

As a result of these factors, they mature later than was previously the case. Although they want to be self-sufficient, and in practice they have more freedom of movement than in the past, the fact is they are less mature and more dependent on adults. In this sense it has been said that many youngsters of our day become more mature in personality but that this happens later than before. The longer period of education and training, and the wider range of information and experience of all kinds open to them, doubtless explain why the level of maturity reached by the youth of today is superior to that of even sixty or seventy years ago. However, the process or the path that leads to that maturity is more difficult and laborious. Today the stage we have called middle adolescence tends to go on for students beyond the age of twenty, thus prolonging the most difficult phase (the phase of impertinence and bad behaviour).

7

The generation gap

1. Group consciousness excludes adults What happens is that young people, whose personality crisis now lasts longer than in the past, finding themselves away from home, without the security that a family provides and without having yet started work, seek support in the peer group. Here they find the security they need and a response to their personal problems. The strong feeling of solidarity among the members makes such groups very compact; the members give one another mutual support and together they can stand up to the adult world. Another notable feature is that these are autonomous groups, for which adolescence is not just a transition period or a passing phase but a complete world with a significance of its own.

Group consciousness among young people today is no longer simply an *esprit de corps* on a local, regional or even national level: it is now something completely international. As P. Laurie says, it is entirely new that, for instance, a girl of fifteen from a small town in Devon should have more points in common with her contemporaries in Tyneside than with her parents or neighbours.[35]

Thus young people have set up their own society, which is outside the society of adults. This makes it extremely difficult for them to attain a responsible level of responsible autonomy and contributes in a major way to the emergence of two present-day facts, namely the proliferation of youth movements and the enormous generation gap. Hence "there is no longer a generation conflict but parallel lives which ignore one another and never meet" (Cruchon, 301).

Apart from the factors just mentioned, this situation is also encouraged by the powerful influence of the modern mass media. Among today's youth, news and opinions circulate very rapidly, thanks to all sorts of reading matter, and radio and television. To this we must add a further fact, namely that nowadays youth is a highly prized element in social life. The need to survive in a changing and competitive society has put two features of the character of youth on a pedestal: their fighting spirit, in other words their determination to overcome obstacles, and their ability to adapt.

2. The influence of the media   The youth of today are much better informed that their predecessors ever were. The press, cinema, radio and television offer a continuous barrage of news, opinion and comment. Much of this chaotic information simply exploits, for commercial purposes, the weaknesses of the teenage personality: the desire to escape, their vulnerability to suggestions from others, their emotional stress and the weak control they have over their imagination, their will or their immediate desires and impulses.

We have seen the important part played by the media in forming the group consciousness of today's youth. We have mentioned that they can also influence physical precociousness, in that they arouse and stimulate sexual interest prematurely. Let us now see some other effects of the media.

The enormous amount of information which young people receive nowadays makes them learn more in breadth than in depth; they certainly know more than before, but very often their knowledge is quite superficial. The large numbers of pictures put before them make it difficult either to concentrate properly on systematic study or to acquire a unified view of what culture is. It must also be said that the messages frequently and openly contradict the facts being taught in the classroom; for instance, teachers often complain that a historical character in a film or on television is not properly researched or is presented against a totally inadequate historical background. Given these circumstances, pupils sometimes call on their extracurricular experience as a basis of "intellectual authority" to argue against a teacher's opinion.

In one way or another the mass media "with their multicoloured variety and their crowded density, are prejudicial to silence, calm and meditation . . . and they fill the adolescents' capacity for experience with material which is not always adequate to their stage of development. Besides . . . the valuable and the valueless are presented to them in one and the same manner and with the same emphasis. Often there is no longer an adult environment that can be said to be educational; there is no public opinion that youth can follow" (Hildebrand, 9).

The surfeit of stimuli projected on to young imaginations, furthermore, gives rise to immoderate flights of fancy. This is all the more so because teenagers have an appetite for the unusual, the weird and even the dangerous. Comics play a decisive role nowadays in the development of the hungry fantasy of our teenagers, encouraging them to action for its own sake and to carry out gratuitous acts.[36] Let us mention, finally, that the mass media, especially the cinema, television and videos, are developing intellectually lazy and passive attitudes in today's youngsters, by continually bombarding them with information that requires little or no thought. They are becoming accustomed to receiving cultural material whether they need it or not and whether they like it or not, without any personal effort or initiative on their part.

3. Effects of social changes It is well known that our society today is above all a changing society, in continual evolution; we are living at a time of ever-accelerating change. For example, we have only to look at urban growth, scientific progress, technological development or the rapidity with which news can travel. Many of these changes are positive signs of advancement in civilization and culture and they bring about better living conditions for mankind. However, at the same time some of these factors do not contribute to our happiness or personal betterment: for instance, the dehumanization of work as a consequence of mass production or the conveyor belt, the massification of the human being, environmental pollution or the increase in man's capacity for self-destruction.

Today's social changes are apparent not only in technical advances and material conditions but also in the sphere of ideas and values. We have all witnessed the loss of a large number of the spiritual and moral values which in earlier periods gave meaning to human life; we have seen confusion and relativism in relation to these values; we have experienced the deterioration of the family . . . . Consequently, today's society does not respond to the needs and aspirations of the adolescent: "In a period invaded by new inventions, technical advances and space adventures, never even imagined by the preceding generation, the old ideas and standards, the old ways of doing things and the values which previously we held to be immutable have totally changed, or are changing so rapidly, that it is difficult for the young person of today to know what he should believe in or practise, nor is he certain any longer of what is worth giving one's life for" (Schneiders, 152).

In preceding ages, the family provided the bridge that allowed the youngster to step from childhood into adulthood with a certain sense of security. Nowadays, in many cases he cannot rely on this support, both because the values of the family have been lost and because there is so little communication and such poor relationships within the home. The rebellious and refractory attitudes of today's youth are due, not so much to any disagreement with adults' ideas and values, as to the sad fact that often such values simply do not exist. They miss those principles, guidelines and models of conduct which they could follow, values personified in the lives of specific individuals who would inspire them to adopt a committed attitude to life.

As a consequence of this situation, "the adolescent of today is in greater conflict with society and with the previous generation. He is in greater disagreement with the demands of authority and he wants more independence. In many cases he is in open rebellion against the exigencies, customs and idols of society. In comparison with the teenagers of the preceding generation, he distances himself from the sanctuary of the home and moves towards the uncertain security of a group of friends" (Schneiders, 156).

The rebellion just mentioned comes from an unsatisfied need for security, from a need to be better guided, from a search for an ideal in which he is not supported by the example or the authority of grown-ups. Little wonder, then, that today's youth should be more sceptical and critical of the adult world, that they should feel anxious and disorientated, that they should be concerned for a more just world and fear the future that awaits them. This fear of the future refers not only to finding steady employment that will suit their aptitudes and preferences, but also and more especially to the fact that society itself has become insecure. Today's youth "are afraid either that the future will not exist at all or that they will not have the personal resources necessary to face the challenges of adult life" (Schneiders, 154). Let us end by adding that, as a consequence of the social changes mentioned, the relationships between parents and teenagers are quite problematical. Teenagers themselves, besides, are difficult to understand.

Part IV:
Three Common Teenage Problems

8

Rebelliousness

1. The rebelliousness of youth   The dictionary defines the verb "to rebel" as "To resist or rise up against a government or other authority". The rebel is therefore "a person who dissents from some accepted moral code or convention of behaviour, dress etc." Rebelliousness is typical of youth and unusual in childhood. It is not that children are never disobedient, but their conduct has a very different significance from that of the teenager. "Before the age of thirteen, the child disobeys through carelessness or in order to refuse something he dislikes. After that age, at fourteen, he disobeys, not because it upsets him to be ordered about, but to protest against the idea of being subordinate to another, as implied in the very notion of obedience. The substance of what he is told is less important to him than the tone of voice of the person giving the orders" (Leif and Delay).[37]

We must distinguish rebelliousness in this sense from obstinacy or stubbornness, from nonconformity or the critical spirit which emerges in middle adolescence. None of these attitudes necessarily implies any rejection of being subordinate to adults. There is no incompatibility between accepting someone's authority in general and differing with him on a particular matter of opinion, even if the discrepancy is persistent and expressed in a stubborn manner. Nevertheless, in so far as such obstinacy and critical spirit are an expression of a teenager's desire for independence, they may tend towards rebelliousness in certain circumstances, which we shall outline later on.

Rebelliousness is also different from violence, even though both often appear side by side. Leif and Delay have studied this difference, and they conclude that violence has no object, implies a complete and total break with others and leads to quite gratuitous acts, while rebelliousness, on the other hand, has an objective (to say no to something), does not break definitively with others, is exercised in the name of something (supports some value) and is never gratuitous.

Rebelliousness, then, is more human than violence.[38]

Juvenile rebelliousness is not always outright or persistent. It takes these forms only in certain cases, as a result of mistaken attitudes on the part of parents or the harmful influence of the environment. On the other hand, isolated symptoms or signs frequently appear throughout adolescence even when the family or the social background has had no harmful influence on the youngster's personality. Whereas in childhood, any wish to dominate is quite instinctive and "childish", "the genuine crisis point of the tendency to impose oneself on others begins to emerge with the awakening of the personality, the awareness of being different from others. Hence we find in young people a jealous feeling of being themselves, an exaggerated way of stressing their own importance, mistrust of what others may say simply because those who say it are others and not themselves" (Guardini, 62).

Within the home, this rebelliousness usually becomes acute between the age of fourteen and seventeen, that is, at the stage which we have said is a time of negative attitudes and impertinence. Outside the family unit, rebelliousness against social customs, values and structures appears later and sometimes continues after the age of twenty, as in the so-called student unrest.

2. Types and causes of rebelliousness   M. Yela distinguishes[39] four types of teenage rebelliousness. The first arises from fear of action and expresses itself in introversion, turning in upon oneself. It is often equivalent to a return to the carefree life devoid of responsibilities typical of childhood; from this refuge, the adolescent adopts an attitude of silent, passive protest against everything. This is *regressive* rebelliousness.

The second is an *aggressive* form of rebelliousness which, unlike the former type, manifests itself in violence. This is typical of the weak person, of someone who cannot bear the difficulties of daily life and tries to alleviate his problem by making others suffer. The third type consists of going against the rules of society, either out of selfishness and self-interest or for the sheer pleasure of flouting them. This is *transgressive* rebelliousness. Finally, there is the *progressive* type, "which is felt as a duty rather than a right. It is not typical of a person who is frightened, weak or amoral. On the contrary, it is a trait of someone who is not afraid of living but wishes to live in a dignified way, who is capable of bearing the weight of reality but not the weight of injustice, who accepts rules made by others but disputes and criticizes them in order to improve them" (Yela, 64).

Two points are worth stressing here: "the *endogenous* factor, caused by the proliferation of the rebelliousness itself and the fear of relapsing into the self-centredness of childhood, and the *exogenous* factor, which appears when the youngster becomes aware that in order to be a man he has to seek a place in society and, to achieve this, he has to compete against adults. Both contribute to the emergence of inner rebelliousness, conflict, rejection, challenge and reaction against grown-ups who force him to study or to work according to their traditions and who watch everything he does. Hence he has the feeling of being on probation" (P. Orive, 58).

The tendency to reject the influence and control of adults first makes itself felt within the family unit. Rebellion against one's parents is the most common and most obvious form, doubtless because their authority is the oldest and has lasted longer than any other. The teenager's first objective, therefore, is to sever his dependence on his parents and cease to be regarded as a child. The rebellious attitude hardens if the desire for independence and self-assertion is met with an over-protective, authoritarian or, indeed, neglectful reaction.

Parents are over-protective when they refuse to admit that the child is growing up and that this process is both physical and mental; they try to prolong his childhood and, consequently, his dependence on them. This makes it difficult for them to trust him, to let him decide things for himself and resolve his own problems, not to "talk down" to him in a superior tone . . . . Parents too often try to go on being indispensable in their child's life, and over-protectiveness is nothing but a form of authoritatianism in disguise.[40]

There are a number of problems associated with authoritarianism. One of these arises when parents exercise their authority arbitrarily, in other words inconsistently, without reference to valid principles or as if exercising a special privilege: the privilege of being parents and adults. This often leads to contradictory standards, for instance, insisting that the child is old enough to do a certain thing on his own and, at other times, that he is not old enough to do the same thing: they tell him to be responsible but yet they treat him as a child. This is the type of authority that "lays down the law", "because I say so" or "because I know best". If this is accompanied by methods that humiliate the child (corporal punishment, reprimands in public, insults etc.), it may provoke an aggressive reaction or feelings of personal frustration, which can aggravate the situation enormously. If parents adopt this kind of dictatorial attitude to their children, it will impede the development of their normal autonomy; they will complain bitterly that they are not treated as human beings but are regarded by their parents as their private property.

On the other hand, disinterest or neglect creates a different problem: in this case no authority of any kind is exercised. The reasons may vary: fear of being regarded as old-fashioned parents, confusing authority with authoritarianism, wanting to have an easy life . . . . Indeed, this last reason, wanting a quiet life, is often the main one nowadays. Despite what one might expect, parents who always allow their children to have their own way also disappoint them and provoke them to rebelliousness. Parental authority provides an essential form of help for them at a time when they find it very hard to help themselves.

After the age of seventeen, rebelliousness frequently spreads beyond the family unit and develops in association with classmates or friends against the whole of society. The earliest manifestations of this type of rebellion were those gangs of youths, the famous "Teddy-boys", who went around committing acts of vandalism.[41] The majority of these young people belonged to quite well-off families. Later on they were emulated by youths in other industrialized countries: the *blousons noirs* in France, the *mambo-boys* in Japan, the *raggare* in Sweden, the *bodgies* in Australia, the *nozem* in Holland . . . . The acts of violence committed by these gangs had no apparent motive; they were simply gratuitous and unprovoked actions: they killed for the sake of killing or robbed for the sake of robbing. Yet "the psychologists and pedagogists discovered a cause: self-assertion through violence was a *symptom of insecurity*. A person who feels secure, with an integrated basis of ideas and emotions, shows no need to assert himself through violence, to make his presence felt in society. He is present and that suffices. Only someone suffering from anxiety or unrest, from an inner conflict which he cannot resolve, needs to explode, to break out" (R. Gómez).[42]

Later on, youth protest reached the students' classrooms and there was a period of student unrest. In their case, the protest was motivated by political factors: university students denounced social injustices and criticized the attempts being made to remedy them. Some of the facts that explain this student unrest are outlined in a description by G. Bonani which, though somewhat lengthy, we feel is worth quoting. "If you want to bring about a student revolt by synthetic means in your laboratory, follow these instructions carefully: take a thousand students . . .; force them to attend lectures in a classroom designed to fit a hundred. Tell them that even if they surmount the hurdle of their examinations there will be no jobs for them. Surround them with a society which does not practise what it preaches, which is governed by parties which do not share the students' ideas. Ask them to think carefully about what is wrong in their society and to suggest remedies. Once they are sufficiently interested in the problem, call in the police to beat them up and throw them out. Then turn up wherever these confrontations are taking place, just in time to express your surprise and bewilderment".[43]

A later form of rebellion was that of the hippies. These protested against society by alienating themselves from it. Behind a justifiable form of apathetic behaviour, with brotherly and pacifist slogans, what these young people were really suffering from was spiritual weariness, a loss of hope, which made them flee both from the social reality around them and from their own personal reality. Life in a commune or taking drugs was — is — a form of escapism for young misfits and unadapted youth.

Having attempted this description of modern youth protest movements, we must ask what motives they all have in common. Undoubtedly the main and most common motive is the deep dissatisfaction that young people feel when faced with a society which they simply dislike and this dissatisfaction actually increases the feeling of insecurity they have in the first place. The youth of today protest against everything and consider themselves a generation of failures because "the myths of the technological society, such as welfare, success and the conquest of power, have disappointed them. The idols presented by their parents are seen to have feet of clay. The traditions of the past have proved inadequate to solve the problems of today" (Bonani, 5).

Basically the youth of today are rebelling against a society of material abundance and spiritual poverty, against the hypocrisy of people who say one thing and do another. They are in bitter disagreement with the adult world and seriously claim the right to set up their own system. Spurred on by the insecurity which present-day society instills into them, they try to find security in their own way but this, in turn, turns out to be the cause of new problems and even greater insecurity.

In this regard, we must ask whether youth has always been a period of rebellion and, if so, whether today's situation is more rebellious or less so than times past.

Young people have always rejected their dependence on their parents and have criticized their world. They have always reacted with hostility to authoritarianism. In a certain sense, these are all symptoms of rebelliousness, but of a normal type and indeed necessary if the individual is to mature and society is to progress. Such expressions of rebelliousness used to last only a short time; they were of an individual type and did not take extremist or radical forms. Starting work at an earlier age, a strong family life and less advanced means of communication were factors that helped to maintain that situation. Besides, there was another special advantage which many societies possessed but which has disappeared today, namely the ability to facilitate the passage from childhood to adulthood in an intelligent and peaceful way. This factor is of considerable importance: "The problem arises from the fact that society today seems to have lost, in general or on average, that ability; once lost, the problems of adolescence spring up more intensely than before. In other words, it is not a problem specific to the youth of today — although there are many such problems — but it has more significance" (Gomez, 9).

We may therefore draw two conclusions: of its very nature, youth is a time of rebellion, but young people today are more rebellious than previously; and their rebellion is more open and expressed more collectively, not because they have changed in any substantive way, but because the society in which they live is different. The rebelliousness of today's youth is rooted in the insecurity of their parents: "There is a 'screw loose' in the people of today. That loose screw, that insecurity about the shape of their future, in other words, about finding some meaning in society or in one's own life, is what causes the greatest feeling of helplessness in the younger generations. ... From whatever angle one tries to define the situation of mankind today, it leads inevitably to the absurd" (Lopez Ibor).[44]

It is only because of certain social changes that the desire for independence on the part of teenagers today takes the form of juvenile delinquency — sometimes seen as a way of "adapting" — or of a marxist-like outlook in the case of some young people who are deeply class conscious vis-a-vis the adult world.

We must not forget, however, that some of today's youth are becoming quite "conformist"; behind the revolutionary language, there lies a bourgeois type of behaviour; they protest against social injustice, but they have no objection to unfairness and selfishness in their own lives. Many degenerate into this attitude because they have never had to struggle to get what they wanted; their lives have been too easy in a permissive society with so many prefabricated products. Hence their rebellion is tainted from the outset by the very faults they criticize in adult society; their rebelliousness is illogical and they have simply inherited it. It is easy to see that this false rebellion presents greater problems of upbringing than the authentic type that comes from genuine dissatisfaction.

3. Some guidelines On the subject of juvenile rebelliousness, as on most other subjects, it is essential to have clear ideas before deciding on the best way to help the youngsters concerned.

First of all, there are certain positive types of rebelliousness which should be accepted and even encouraged. "Rebellion is neither to be tossed off as 'just adolescence', to be laughed at, to be infuriated by, or to be cried over . . . . It needs to be understood as unpleasant evidence that a natural desire to grow up, to become a self-sustaining individual in one's own right, is being sought, albeit in a very awkward fashion" (Gallagher and Harris).[45]

Secondly, we must distinguish genuine rebelliousness from other attitudes and forms of behaviour which are not rebellious. Far too often a youngster is labelled a rebel simply because he has opinions of his own, says what he thinks or acts in accordance with his own principles.

Thirdly, each case and each situation must be dealt with individually. Youngsters are above all people: being a rebel is something "accidental" and may have different causes in each case. There are no universal panaceas to cure this problem. Before taking any steps, therefore, we must find out what each individual is rebelling against and why. Rebelliousness within the family, resulting from exacerbated feelings of independence as a reaction to authoritarian parents, is obviously easier to deal with than that which goes beyond the limits of the home, forming part of a wider revolt against society or the adult world in general.

There is no point in trying to deal with rebellion within the family by adopting a condescending or paternalistic attitude. To put on a superior air and say to a child, "Let's have a chat" or to use this strategem as a way out of a difficult situation is just as bad as not talking to him at all. He needs to be understood and loved without being patronized and he wants to be treated differently from others. Above all, he wants to be regarded as an adult, even though he is not yet one strictly speaking. He will feel that he is being treated as an adult when grown-ups expect and demand of him more than they expect of children. Obviously this attitude is not incompatible with common sense and ordinary prudence, which will not burden young shoulders with weights that are too heavy or dangerous.

He will also feel he is being treated as an adult when grown-ups no longer confine their dealings with him to issuing orders, forbidding things, giving him advice or telling him what to do, but also, and more importantly, listen to him, take his ideas into account, let him act on his own initiative and take him seriously.

The fact that he rejects the idea of being subordinate to his parents, together with the suggestions we have just made on how to treat him as an adult, may prompt the question whether obedience can, in fact, be demanded of an adolescent. According to the law, of course, children are subject to their parents until they come of age. In this sense, therefore, they can certainly be required to obey. However, legal arguments scarcely provide the best way of influencing children. To answer the question sensibly, we must distinguish between blind, passive obedience and intelligent, active obedience. It is understandable that the former kind should irritate any youngster, for it amounts to his abdicating all use of his own free will; it is a degraded type of obedience, which is quite unnecessary once he has discovered motives for his obedience, once he has decided to do what he has to do freely, because it is right or because it is the best thing. This form of obedience is perfectly compatible with the use of one's own initiative and intelligence in making decisions.[46]

To avoid the danger of regarding obedience as something solely for children, it is essential to try and get youngsters to recognize authority before they agree to submit to it. This approach "is closer to the adult approach which, though obeying laws, prefers to use different terminology to explain why it breaks them". Furthermore, if "submission to parental authority is presented to the child as related to his social situation and a consequence of a contract to which he is a party, perhaps he will find it easier to understand" (Favez-Boutonier).[47]

Rebelliousness outside the family is more complicated and difficult to handle because the factors which cause it are partly beyond the control of the parents and others involved. They cannot transform society immediately or on their own initiative by imbuing it with all the values it lacks; while it is true that they can and should influence society for the better, it is nevertheless unlikely that the results of their efforts will affect their own children directly.

One promising way to deal with this problem is to try to get the youngsters to convert their sterile, ineffective protest and criticism, their apathy and violence, into a form of rebellion that will attack the defects and deficiencies of today's society in a more constructive way, approaching them as a challenge for their own improvement rather than as an excuse for an easy life or for continuing with their negative, irresponsible conduct.

Closely related with this point is the importance of not making it too easy for them to achieve everything they want. On the contrary, it is better to create situations in which they will have to make some effort to achieve results; they will learn to value something if it has to be earned, if it requires personal sacrifice and effort.

The object is to get them to opt for the *progressive* type of rebellion, "the constructive, not the destructive, type, the kind that feeds on love and not on hatred, that unites rather than divides, that belongs to the new man, exercising his new and still pure freedom, who wants to act so as to make others more free" (Yela, 64).

An example of this approach might be to suggest to youngsters that they should opt for reflection and a critical sense, and set themselves against the superficiality and monotony of contemporary society. Joseph Pieper sees in contemplation a questioning of oneself concerning the true meaning of things, and this is a pressing need for youngsters who face a society losing the meaning of individual and community life; it is also one of the major contributions that one can make to the good of those who make up that society. Hence we should encourage them to "rebel against superficiality and restore the exercise of the intelligence."[48]

The rebelliousness of youth should be encouraged to swim against the current, rejecting a type of culture "based on the separation of freedom, truth and love" (Gómez, 154) by trying to unite these three factors in one's own life. It will be all the easier to encourage this responsible, constructive kind of rebellion, leading to the betterment of oneself and others, if parents and teachers can take advantage of the youngsters' excessive energy and channel it towards activities that are fully meaningful for them. At this age, it is essential to find stimulating and interesting jobs for them to do, something that will increase their experience and culture, and get them to carry out some project or help others, and launch them on such activities.

Their desire to be treated as adults may also be utilized to suggest to them something along the following lines: A person has a right to be treated as a grown-up when he acts as one and not as a child, and adults are able to govern themselves, control themselves and assume responsibility for their own development.

If youngsters are to progress towards the attainment of this goal, specific objectives like the following might be proposed to them:

— They should become more sincere with themselves and try to see themselves as they really are: cease to deceive themselves and attempt to discover their main faults;

— They should learn to control their personal impulses and use them in the service of noble ideals;

— They should discover more ideals and values (fortitude, resilience, courage, fidelity, justice) in living people or historical characters; on discovering each value, they should reflect on it and make concrete resolutions to act according to its demands.

9

Leaving home

1. Running away from home Adolescents have always run away from home, but at the present time the incidence of this has increased considerably as a result of the deterioration of the family and the social environment. Typical of today, furthermore, is the high number of "pseudo-escapes" from home, and these take many forms*. The problem is especially worrying nowadays because of the group consciousness which has recently come into existence among youngsters: "In the 1950s, the majority of teenagers who ran away from home usually returned, because they had nowhere to go. From the 1960s onwards, far fewer return: they are nearly always taken in and sheltered by a gang of friends" (Orive, 58).

Running away from home satisfies a need to get away from an environment in which the young person feels uncomfortable. Normally it is not based on a conscious decision, especially at the age of puberty — but on an impulsive desire to get away, with no specific destination in mind and with little thought for the possible consequences of such action. It usually happens quite unexpectedly — the parents are always taken by surprise — and very often it is of short duration, except in cases of the kind just mentioned, where the fugitive is taken in by a gang of friends or when it occurs at the end of the middle stage or during the later stage of adolescence. In many such cases, the youngsters are able to take care of themselves and may stay away for longer periods.

It is interesting that the "culprits" have no sense of guilt for what they have done. "On their return — usually brought back by a member of the family or by a police officer — they show no sign of repentance, no sorrow, just as if they had simply tasted a moment's freedom or

*G. Cruchon provides an enlightening note related to his own country: "According to official figures published in 1966, in the previous seven years there was an average of 2,500 adolescents per year who ran away from home, that is, seven per day" (op. cit. 180).

taken a few deep breaths of independence for a little while. The escape calms them down" (Mucchielli).[49] Leaving home physically, running away, is a typical reaction of early adolescence, whereas more symbolic escapes or "pseudo-escapes" are more usual in middle adolescence.

Many possible interpretations of escaping from home have been put forward: a show of protest against the family atmosphere, a stratagem to avoid some punishment, a yearning for adventure or for the unknown, an attempt to deal with new situations or to resolve one's problems on one's own. It is no longer regarded exclusively as the behaviour of irresponsible, abnormal or delinquent youngsters. In France, for example, it is not considered to be a criminal offence, even though it is acknowledged that, if prolonged, it may lead initially to vagrancy and later even to crime. In fact, to treat this as an offence might make a criminal of someone who, in principle, only has a problem of immaturity or incompatibility with his family.

2. Forms of escape from home   The most common type of escape from home consists of physically running away. It is usually something quite spontaneous and done unthinkingly, especially at the age of puberty. In middle adolescence, on the other hand, it is sometimes premeditated: "Under pressure from a problematical and difficult environment, adolescents spend days, months or even years harbouring the thought of running-away. When they see clearly that their situation has no solid basis, they implement it as the only way to freedom" (Orive, 342). A feature of the premeditated escape is that there has been a plan to save some money or to find a job so to be able to live away from home.

There is another type of escape in which the youngster does not physically leave home, but nevertheless is morally miles away from it and feels totally cut off from the family environment. It is not unusual in this case for the individual to take refuge in a dream world made to suit himself.

Nowadays there are more and more escapes from home but "covered up" or disguised. We have referred to these as "pseudo-escapes" and, although they do not involve an open or total break with the family, nevertheless in practice they often mean leaving home for good. The youngster looks for a job or some socially acceptable excuse to leave the family: to work somewhere else, to join the army, to share a flat with other students, to live in a hostel, etc.

The seriousness of what we have called "being morally miles away" should not be underestimated. "Physical escapes from home are relatively few . . . . However, the state of 'passive rebellion', expressions of indiscipline, refusal to perform one's obligations and 'long faces' are much more frequent, and these pass unnoticed. They form the basis of subsequent physical escapes and are often used as a means of blackmail to leave school and get a job . . . . (Orive, 346).

3. Common reasons for leaving home   There are various reasons for leaving home. Some are closely connected with unhappy social or family circumstances: marriages that have broken down physically or morally, rows between parents, lack of affection in the home, etc. Among unfavourable psychological conditions in the home that encourage the thought of escaping from it, we may mention boarding-school life if cut off from the family, resentment caused by second marriages and hostile or unfair treatment of one child in comparison with the others.[50]

Family pressures are another frequent cause: authoritarianism, patronizing attitudes or over-rigidity on the part of parents. Such forms of pressure, in the children's eyes, are a serious obstacle to their personal autonomy. In such an atmosphere, failure in an examination or fear of punishment may be sufficient motive for leaving home. This may sometimes be simply a way of searching for something new, something different or unknown or of returning to some "special place". In this case, the individual merely wants to return to a place from which in the first he was taken away or expelled, a place which is often associated with a person, a pet animal or some special spot in the landscape (a road, a tree, a house) especially vivid in his memory.[51]

A predisposition to leave home is frequently intensified by some mental deficiency or personality defect. Nervous children, for instance, may run away spontaneously just because of a family row. Others do so because of a feeling of inferiority; an escape from home always indicates some emotional regression, which shows that there was insufficient love.

Another factor that may play a decisive role in bringing about this problem is the harmful influence of others: for instance, he may meet someone else who has already left home.

4. Keeping teenagers at home   On the question of how parents should prevent their children from running away from home, it is most important, first of all, that they should realize that the problem is seriously on the increase at the present time. They should be aware of the various causes of the problem and understand that these causes may arise even in the best of family backgrounds: for instance, those connected with the child's own personality or the harmful influence of the environment. They should also be aware of the grave dangers involved in allowing a child to stay away from home unsupervised for any length of time; especially if prolonged, this situation can lead to contact with people of all types, wandering around or stealing as a livelihood; leaving home may give rise to juvenile delinquency.

Parents should also be aware that the most serious cases of running away are not in early adolescence but in the middle stage. At the age of puberty there are only physical escapes, which are usually unpremeditated and brief. After about the age of fifteen, however, the move can be moral as well as physical and, although less frequent than in the earlier period, it is more often premeditated and lasts longer. There are also the "pseudo-escapes" or those that are "covered up".

Obviously on this point prevention is not only better, but also easier, than cure, and it must be done primarily in the home. The family climate must be a healthy one if the teenager is to adapt to it properly. Therefore it is important to ask oneself in each case to what extent family relationships are favourable to each child's basic need to develop individually, to feel secure and be accepted.

From his earliest years, the child gains courage and strength from the self-confidence inspired in him by being an integral part of a family, and this comes from feeling that he is unconditionally accepted, that he is loved, not because he is useful or good at something, not for any qualities which others might also have, but because of what he is himself: unique, different from others, a person unlike any other. This is precisely the difference between family and the social envionment: outside the family, he is accepted only in so far as he fulfils certain conditions and serves a purpose. There is always the danger of accepting one's children conditionally, that is, provided they do certain things, behave in a certain way or are good at something. If this happens, the unique, singular and individual character of the person is ignored; the personal sense of the human relationship is lost and is replaced in terms of social interests and functions.

The child's feeling of integration within the family also depends on whether he is treated as a "perfectable" human being, as someone who can improve and make progress. Leonardo Polo defines man as a perfecting being who perfects himself and adds that this definition fits in with the Christian sense of love: a hopeful love. Relationships are different depending on whether something is expected of people or not, whether they are respected (in spite of their defects) or rejected. In this regard there are two extremes to be avoided: either pressurizing them or neglecting them. Some demands should be made on them, for hope always makes demands and someone who can improve should do so, but any demands should take account of the individual's potential.

Attitudes like these, involving unconditional acceptance and trust in the children or teenagers, are diametrically opposed to those factors that drive them away from home: family pressures, undue severity, intolerance of their mistakes or failures, lack of affection and coldness between parents and children. Parents should therefore ask themselves whether they are capable of allowing their child to be as he is, of waiting patiently, of loving him with a totally unselfish and "tangible" love, in other words, love that he can see and feel in concrete examples.

The child will also be helped to feel settled and secure within the family if the parents know and encourage his ambitions and help him in his problems — one of the main areas being his study or work — just as he too should be involved in the family chores and even worries. This will mean keeping him informed of everything that affects him, asking his opinion whenever necessary and giving him an opportunity to contribute to the "family success" through his own efforts. These attitudes play a part in consolidating the unity and harmony of the family and "building the home together". When this is done, it ceases to be a boring, uneasy place, and begins to offer its occupants something new every day.

Since one of the possible causes of leaving home is the influence of friends and companions — either by encouraging a child to abandon his family or by giving him a place to stay after the event — it is easy to see how important it is that parents should know their children's friends. Hence we repeat that for this reason the home should be open to them at all times.

Finally, let us say that the best prevention of this particular problem is that parents should show great understanding of the mistakes and the needs of their teenage children and give them ever opportunity to think, to express their opinions and act freely. Teenagers need to know and feel that their parents trust them and love them, not with a protective or stiffling affection, but with an open, generous love, willing to make personal sacrifices. This will help them to "exercise watchfulness over the adolescent from a distance. It suffices that he should know that his parents are there if he should need them. They must let him come and go . . . without binding him to the home with iron shackles . . . . Coercion, force or inflexible attitudes will only drive him further away from those who create this atmosphere and force him to resort to leaving home, with all the dangers that result from that" (Orive, 353).

10

Shyness and feelings of inferiority

1. Shyness We all know people — children, teenagers and adults — who are incapable of sitting in the front row when they arrive late for a show, are unable to claim their rights in any situation, try not to cross a room if it means attracting attention or prefer to write rather than speak face to face. If a person behaves habitually like this, we have a classical case of shyness.

Shyness is a feeling of being unable to do anything in the presence of others. It is chronic fear of action and comes from lack of confidence in others and in oneself. A shy person does not dare present himself to others as he really is, for fear of creating a bad impression of himself. Shyness, therefore, arises from attaching undue importance to the opinion of others. It consists of a duplication of the ego between actor and spectator. The shy person believes and feels that he is always being watched. He projects on to others his own observation of himself, he thinks they see him as he sees himself; he feels threatened and critized. Hence shyness is insecurity provoked by being looked at.

The effects and consequences of shyness are also well known. In the company of others, the shy person appears to shrink away; he is ashamed, mentally confused, awkward in expression. In extreme cases, the situation may lead to acute anguish and even to momentary loss of one of the mental faculties. Fear, and then the fear of being afraid, causes the individual more and more to avoid all situations which could cause it, until almost his whole life becomes paralysed. This obsessive idea invades his consciousness, making it impossible for a shy person to come out of himself and assert himself effectively in life.

The shy person is extremely worried by the external effects of his shyness because often they cause the very thing he most wished to avoid — being noticed and watched by others. However, this need not invariably be a problem. Only when it goes too far does it seriously disturb the mental and emotional life of the person affected so as to create a permanent state of anxiety and unrest. If it is not too acute, it may cause no worry, though, of course, this will depend on personal circumstances of all kinds: age, level of intelligence, type of job etc.

The problem tends to appear between the second and third stages of childhood (beteen the age of five and seven). At this age children are not yet afraid of others but they may, in fact, be afraid of themselves. They are shy almost unconsciously and it is more physical than psychic. In adolescence it becomes much more conscious and systematic; whereas a child may be shy but is unaware of what this means, the teenager will know he is shy and will realize the significance this may have for his entire life. Shyness is not something exclusive to adolescence but that this is the normal age for it. The adolescent is shy by nature.

One reason why shyness is more usual in adolescents than in children is that their ability to think and reflect allows them to analyse themselves and "stand back" from themselves; they become aware of their own shyness, and this awareness is in fact the main cause of the problem. A second important reason is that teenagers have to face the problem of adjusting to new environments. As children, they lived in a relatively easy and favourable atmosphere: they had no great worries provided they were obedient and docile to the ideas and habits passed on to them by grown-ups. Adolescents, on the other hand, have ideas of their own and this makes them more inclined to doubt and mistrust themselves and others.

One might think, then, that this difficulty of adjusting during adolescence is essentially dangerous and should be avoided if possible. Similarly one might consider it is desirable that youngsters in early adolescence should be fully adjusted to their environment, with complete trust in themselves and others. But the fact is that adolescents of fifteen to eighteen years of age who are too sure of themselves, and feel no unease in the company of the opposite sex or strangers, still retain something of their childish mentality. Their security may be a sign of underdevelopment; at best, they are likely to become mediocre adults who will be satisfied to evade difficulties simply because their lack of originality allows them to adjust effortlessly to social conditions which, of their very nature, are appropriate only to average minds.

However, there is a danger that difficulty in adjusting to new circumstances may lead to immaturity, rather than to maturity. It is just as risky to be unaware of difficulties as to be overawed by them. In practice, there are many cases of adolescent shyness leading to mental illnesses which leave the individual suffering from shyness all his adult life.

2. Shyness and feelings of inferiority From what we have said it will be clear that shyness and feelings of inferiority are closely related. We have seen that shyness is a chronic fear, involving mistrust of oneself and others, and is rooted in a sense of insecurity. This association accounts for the fact that some writers on the subject treat shyness and inferiority feelings as synonymous, although in fact the relationship is one of cause and effect: awkwardness in dealing with others is a result of feeling insecure. Not infrequently consciousness of being awkward aggravates the initial insecurity.

Shyness and feelings of inferiority, although different, feed off one another all the time: anything which causes a feeling of inferiority is a cause of shyness or, at least, encourages it; undoubtedly, shyness is nothing other than awareness of one's inferiority. This gives rise to clumsiness and bashfulness, which are simply the external symptoms of shyness and aggravate it.

To go a little more deeply into this question, we must distinguish three concepts: a feeling of inferiority, an inferiority complex and the "knowledge that one is inferior".

We all know we are inferior to others in some particular ability or expertise and to acknowledge this fact is no reason for any trauma or maladjustment. On the contrary, it usually stimulates us to personal improvement. A feeling of insecurity, on the other hand, involves seeing oneself solely and exclusively in terms of one's defects and limitations. Therefore this feeling means grossly exaggerating one's awareness of some personal inferiority. In fact, the defect being seen in such disproportionate terms is not always even real: it may be quite imaginary. In any case, inferiority feelings usually arise from some problem created by the individual rather and have no objective basis.

Obviously if a person suffers from a feeling of inferiority, he is conscious of it, for otherwise the feeling would not exist. This does not apply, however, to the so-called "inferiority complex" which always relates to the subconscious; even when it exercises a decisive influence on his behaviour, he is still unaware of its existence.

Due to the theories of Adler, perhaps, too much importance has been attached to the feeling of inferiority; it is sometimes seen as the whole issue, when in fact it is only one element among many in the psychology of the individual. Some experts now consider that an awareness of inferiority is not even necessarily harmful in adults; indeed it may be a starting point for enriching the personality. This is not the case with the adolescent, however; for him it may be traumatic and quite damaging. Young people cannot accept a feeling of inferiority.[53] If they cannot overcome it, they experience inner

79

suffering which nearly always turns into acute shyness, cowardice, rebelliousness or neurosis. It also tends to lead them to seek inappropriate psychological compensations which involve certain dangers.

By compensation we mean the self-regulatory effect, common to all living beings, which tends to restore any balance that has been upset.[54] In the case of the adolescent, we can distinguish emotional from social compensations. The former usually take the form of angry reactions, even involving violence, and states of depression: melancholy and passive periods etc. Social compensation can be more dangerous. Here the youngster tries to conceal or disguise his inferiority by various means and at the same time seeks the respect and admiration of others. He may, for instance, try to cover up his defect with some fictitious virtue: this is the case with the "cocky" youngster. Or he may deliberately attract attention by using "bad language" or wearing outrageous or slovenly clothes.

Lying or stealing may also be forms of social compensation. The teenager tells lies, not to avoid physical pain (as he did when he was a child), but to avoid moral suffering for example, some humiliating punishment. A lie told by way of compensation consists of hiding the truth from a particular person, precisely because it would be used to degrade him.[55] In the case of stealing, the object stolen attempts to substitute "mine" for "me".[56]

Leaving home can also be a form of psychological compensation whereby the youngster runs away from the social circumstances which are the cause of his inferiority.

The feeling of insecurity arises when the young person discovers that grown-ups have certain abilities which he does not possess. It may be considerably heightened if he finds that they are habitually dissatisfied with his way of doing things. However, when the educational and social environments are not unfavourable, this feeling normally disappears as he grows up.

3. Common causes of feelings of inferiority Although the normal age for the onset of shyness is during adolescence, as we have said, this may also appear earlier, in childhood. If a child is shy, his problems of insecurity tend to increase as he enters his teens.

Shyness in childhood is practically always caused by improper attitudes and methods of upbringing on the part of the parents. One such attitude is over-protection, as when some mothers stop their children from taking a single step on their own and solve all their problems for them, so that they take no risks themselves. The children then have no opportunity to develop their own abilities, and the first time they have to face a difficulty without their mother being present they feel unable to cope with it.

Another attitude not to be recommended is that of those mothers who show off their children in front of visitors by getting them to perform: to sing, dance, tell a story etc. It is quite normal for a child to do something well and willingly for his family and yet do the same thing badly or not at all in the presence of others. This is not because he wants to shame his mother but simply because he finds it embarrassing to perform in public. Neither is it due to shyness, at least in principle, although this may arise if the mother goes on forcing him in each new situation, for such pressure will make him feel a failure.

An attitude not related to this is to make excessive demands on children, whether at home or at school. A mother who expects her daughter to be able to embroider as well as she does and the teacher who gets angry at every slight mistake are both sowing the seeds of inferiority feelings. This may emerge in adolescence: "It comes to the surface again in adolescence, a new phase, fragile and inclined to introversion and self-consciousness, when the young person feels awkward, uneasy in the presence of grown-ups, when his physical appearance and his image of himself do not measure up to his expectations, when his companions once again seem to have little respect for him and make jokes at his expense" (Cruchon, 318).

Maladjustment to physical and mental changes in puberty gives rise to a constant feeling of insecurity, and this becomes even more acute if adults make undue demands on them. When they see how their children have developed physically, parents often expect them to behave like grown-ups, forgetting that psychological development usually lags far behind physical growth. Adolescents are very sensitive, besides, to physical defects and humiliating situations. It can aggravate their feeling of inferiority if any mistake they have made is told in public, if they are compared to unattractive characters or punished in some way that hurts their pride.

4. Prevention and cure   Prevention is better than cure in the case of shyness, as in other things; at least, it is better to ensure that the problem does not become acute or incurable. Prevention begins at birth and goes on until puberty.

Parents and teachers should avoid habitual severity and intolerance, continuously saying no, offering unnecessary help, making excessive demands or humiliating comparisons and punishments. "Children should be surrounded with understanding and kindness. Shyness in adolescents, more than anything else, comes from insufficient effort on the part of adults to understand and be kind to the child and, above all, to show him that he is understood" (Lacroix, 179).

Another point is that shyness and awkwardness are closely related. "Shy people are often terribly awkward: they are unable to use physical objects. Awkwardness is the result of shyness and at the same time aggravates it . . . . Children should be taught to use objects and to be skilful" (Lacroix, 173). To prevent shyness children should be accustomed, gradually and without undue pressure, to do things in the presence of others; this will make them less likely to be afraid in public. It may also help them to avoid feeling isolated and out of place, as so often happens with shy people, if they are given tasks or jobs to do with some social implications.

To overcome the problem, the first step must be an attempt to find its causes. This means identifying the defect, real or imaginary, to which the individual is attaching disproportionate importance. Once this is done, the real nature of his problem should be explained to him and he should be convinced that the deficiency which is worrying him so much is either totally imaginary or in no way makes him inferior to others on an overall basis. There is no need — nor is it even desirable — to conceal whatever faults or limitations he may have. The best thing is to tell him the truth, pointing out that his deficiency is not as important as he thinks. It may also encourage him to know that others with similar difficulties have been successful and happy in life; this will help him to come to terms with himself as he really is, with his good and bad qualities, and his limitations will cease to be an insurmountable obstacle in his way.

Coming to terms with himself does not mean resigning himself to remaining as he is. On the contrary, it should be the starting point, the launching pad, to go on to better things. It is essential that he be convinced that his shyness can be cured and that this depends above all on his own determination to overcome it.

Since his problem stems from a feeling of insecurity, his self-confidence should be built up all the time. This can be achieved by continually showing him abilities which he scarcely knew he possessed, helping him to develop other skills to compensate for those he lacks, exploiting some strong point or some good quality of his and providing him with opportunities for success in situations where we know he can excel.

In a Canadian documentary on shyness,[57] there is a sequence in which a teacher cures a pupil's shyness when she notices that she can dance; the development of this ability gives the girl the self-confidence she needs. Another example is that of a teacher asking a shy pupil the questions which he is fairly sure he can answer correctly.

Shyness is something that cannot be overcome without a personal effort on the part of the individual concerned. This involves strengthening his will by gradually doing things in particular situations: "While others can do a great deal for people suffering from shyness, they can also do a great deal for themselves . . . The shy person is so afraid, so undaring, that he cannot live a normal life. Yet his experience tells him that every time he throws off his fear and dares to do something, he feels happy and satisfied, whatever the outcome . . . . Let him dare! Let him undertake difficult tasks, and little by little he will strengthen his indecisive will" (Lacroix, 184).

It is also worth suggesting to him that he should give up taking refuge in that pride of his: as Lacroix says, he cannot be humble and shy at the same time (ibid., 186).

Another quality to be recommended is concern for people: this will encourage him to come out of himself. "Every time a shy person does a good deed for someone, he does it for himself . . . . His best moments are when he is doing something for others" (ibid., 187f).

We may sum up our recommended treatment for shyness and feelings of inferiority, then, by saying that the adult has two functions, namely to make demands (but with understanding) and to encourage self-confidence; the youngster, for his part, should lay the stress on: knowledge and acceptance of himself, personal effort, humility and social openness.

11

Study

Obviously this is a subject that needs attention, not only in the teenage years but also earlier, in the second and third stages of childhood, that is from the age of six to nine and from ten to twelve, approximately. Indeed at every age study poses specific problems to be faced in the context of overall education and development. However, it seems that difficulties arise in adolescence which are more closely related to personality. As well as the other profound and complex changes taking place at this stage within the child, the subjects studied are becoming more difficult and the end of compulsory education is approaching (involving the decision whether to stay on at school or to start work). The dangers from harmful influence of the environment are greater than before.

Let us consider study and work by examining two particular dangers which can, and do, arise, namely an obvious deterioration in school work and the question of leaving school early.

These two points are not unrelated, because a poor school performance is usually an essential factor in deciding not to continue one's education. While poor results are not the prerogative of teenagers, the danger of giving up full-time education is (this question does not arise until the school-leaving age is reached). In dealing with the possible causes of these two problems, we shall have to mention the matter of money and ask to what extent the parents' and children's attitudes to financial affairs alleviates or aggravates the difficulties (see Chapter 15).

1. Causes and effects of poor school performance A deterioration in school work is a common problem among adolescents. Their results tend to be worse than previously and they feel less at ease in the school environment; for example, they may complain for the first time about the teachers, examinations, discipline, school rules etc. Not all are affected to the same extent, of course; individual cases range from downright failure to others where the work scarcely shows any difference. The variation from one person to another is due to such factors as: the child's basic understanding of each subject, his study methods, whether the education at primary level has been a help or a hindrance for adolescence, the extent to which the teenage crisis affects him and whether the home and the school climate help or hinder his study in some way.

A serious danger for parents and teachers alike is that they may attribute poor work simply to laziness and act accordingly. Of course, there are lazy teenagers — indeed we might say that all teenagers are to some extent lazy when compared with earlier stages — but it would be wrong to attribute a complex problem like this to a single cause. Such over-simplification may even aggravate the difficulty and lead to other problems that may cause conflict between parents and children. Parents and teachers should therefore investigate the specific causes of the situation and try to get a proper understanding of the difficulty in each particular case.

First of all, it must be stressed that, especially in the early stage, that is to say at puberty, the teenager does indeed feel lazy. Obviously the organic changes that he undergoes between the ages of twelve and fourteen approximately, especially his height and the appearance of primary and secondary sexual characteristics, together with the instability of his feelings and his changes of interests, are the reasons why he no longer feels the same towards his work as he did at the end of his childhood, for instance. It is not unusual for a teenager to feel quite tired after doing something which his teachers may believe requires an effort well within his capabilities, or he may find it difficult to concentrate on his work simply because something that happened during the day has hurt his feelings.

Secondly, the adolescent is going through a period of conflict. He clashes with the values of his childhood, with the values of grown-ups and even with himself, in that he has to adjust to a newly-discovered personality, beginning with an attempt to understand himself and learning to cope with new and more difficult situations than ever before. Open confrontation with others will be less likely or less violent if his earlier upbringing helps him to deal with the crisis, but nevertheless there is always some re-examination of the values, principles and rules learned in childhood. This background of conflict has a decisive influence on the teenager's school work because not only does it make it impossible for him to concentrate fully but also the old rules and methods are replaced by new ones.

The development of certain mental aptitudes may also have

repercussions on his studies. The change from purely mechanical memorizing to the associative type of memory often causes difficulties in learning, at least at the beginning, because the pupil is using an underworked faculty. We might also mention that it is more difficult to pay attention, due to the emergence of new interests and problems and the development of the imagination, with the tendency to day-dream, which makes him take refuge in a world of fantasy so as to evade the worries and responsibilities of the real world.

The pupil's own motives for studying are very important. For this reason great attention should be paid to the development of his interests from childhood into the teenage years. A child is curious about everything around him, but as he gets older he becomes interested in fewer things. It is not that his interests actually disappear but that he puts more energy into fewer of them. This is why it seems that teenage interests are concentrated and specialized; concerns of a social, philosophical or religious type predominate over the more concrete matters of earlier stages. This development affects the use of the intellect and may cause a certain lack of interest in school work. Hence it is normal for teenage pupils to feel more attracted towards those school subjects they think will be most useful and relevant for life and to lose interest in the others — usually the majority! They tend to think that these others are unnecessary and a mere waste of time. Naturally this drop in motivation is further complicated if the teaching methods are boring, if the school organization is over-rigid or if the teachers demand more than they should reasonably expect.

The cumulative effect of past academic failures and gaps in the learning of certain subjects may be decisive for the learning process during the teenage years. At primary school the consequences of this would have been less serious because, not only was the depth and breadth of the subjects themselves substantially less, but also anything that went unlearned had less of a "snowball effect" on other subjects. At secondary level, however, the pupil has the problem of keeping up with everything taught and making up for anything missed — which may be a lot and may be quite important.

In the light of these considerations, it is easy to see why so many adolescents regard school as nothing but a legal formality or a boring duty imposed on them by their parents, involving endless classes, countless examinations and detestable exercises. Hence for many of them it is something to be finished as quickly as possible; they find it much more sensible and attractive to look for a job that will earn them some money immediately, so that they can buy wheels and take out a girl-friend or boy-friend at the week-ends.

2. Guidelines It must be stressed from the outset that these difficulties, caused by the development of the personality, are by no means disastrous for school work, because what the child brings forward from his earlier experience (habits of study, good behaviour etc.) may still be of great importance. Most of the problems involved tend to be transitory or to affect only some areas: they never affect the whole person or the whole curriculum. Nevertheless, there is a risk of profound and lasting maladjustment if parents or teachers interpret poor performance as a kind of defiance: "he refuses to do any work", "she only wants to annoy us" etc. This gives rise to a state of war, which may cause an emotional blockage in some youngsters, systematic rebellion in others, and may result in their leaving school before they should. Parents should try to realize that the problem cannot be resolved from outside the child — by means of rewards and punishments, for example — but only from inside him; this involves finding out the specific causes, telling him about them and working out some plan that can be put into practice with his collaboration. The role of the parents in this matter may be summarized in five points:

— Stimulate and motivate the child to study;
— Make demands, but with great understanding;
— Provide facilities for him to study at home and try to get him to do so efficiently;
— Give the child good advice on the proper use of his free time.

It is important to motivate pupils at every stage of their education, but parents and teachers should make special efforts during adolescence: we have only to think of the difficulties outlined above. Rather than merely offering them material incentives, it is much better to motivate them to see the importance of their study and of doing it responsibly, with perseverance and effort. The object is to get them to assimilate and "take to heart" those values related to work well done. In childhood the main aim was to get the child to acquire the habit of work, but in adolescence priority has to be given to instilling personal convictions so that work will be seen and done as a means of making oneself a better person.[58] Parents should stimulate their children's curiosity and present study as a search for answers to questions worked out in advance. It is particularly advisable in motivating pupils to attach more importance to effort than to results and to give good example in the parents' own work. For instance, they should examine their own motives for working, asking themselves whether they do it merely to earn money or whether they have higher motives; they should also ask themselves whether they complain in front of the children about having too much work to do.

The five points mentioned above are all connected with motivating children to study properly. To make demands on them in an understanding way, involves knowing and taking account of each child's potential and limitations, so as to expect neither more nor less than he can give. Therefore parents should be less concerned about a "good performance" (by comparing the results obtained with the objective standard set by the teacher) than about "satisfactory performance" (comparing them with the effort actually made and the pupil's ability). To do this, they need sufficient information about their child and his way of working, including knowledge of the nature and problems of adolescence. This information may be acquired through the teachers, but also through the child himself provided there is a good relationship with him.

The provision of facilities at home means creating proper conditions and a good atmosphere so that the work can be done in some comfort, without interruptions, in a place and in surroundings which will encourage concentration and motivate proper study. This will involve points like not switching on the television during study time, making an effort to have some silence in the house, not sending the child on errands when he is studying . . . . Parents should also take an interest in the way he studies, because his method, as well as his ability and the effort he makes, are vital factors in his performance at school. This is especially important when we realize how common it is for children not to know how to study properly, because they receive no guidance from their early years and they get into more and more bad habits that hinder their work (learning by rote, passive study, bad organization of their time, failure to set themselves specific aims etc.), and this is a serious obstacle to the learning process.

There are many ways in which parents can help and guide their children. For instance, they could give them a book on how to study; speak to the teachers about this problem, and tell them of any bad habits noticed at home so that they can try to correct them at school; or simply themselves give good advice to their children based on what they learn either from the teachers or from reading about this important subject. This kind of cooperation with teachers is all the more important if a child has any special difficulty with particular subjects due to some basic deficiency, such as gaps carried forward from previous years; in these cases it is advisable to make a concrete plan to rectify the difficulties, such as special periods of study, special tuition etc.

Learning to use one's free time properly is closely connected with school work because whatever the child does outside of his study hours may be a help or a hindrance. His leisure activities may be educational or not, depending on how the child regards them and on parental guidance. A common danger is sheer idleness, which leads to bad habits (untidiness, passivity, lack of effort etc.). Teachers know that their pupils are noticeably less well disposed towards work after the holidays; therefore parents should ensure that they are busy during their free time and that even purely recreational activities should involve some effort and some demands being made on them. They should also keep a check on what they read, on their friends and pastimes, for these may be as damaging to their study as they are to other aspects of their conduct.

3. Leaving school early: causes and remedies Many teenagers leave school when they could, or should, stay on. Apart from pupils who are not particularly suited to study and for whom a job might be the right decision, there are many who are sufficiently bright to benefit from further education but waste their talents by leaving. This is a very worrying decision for parents because the children are interrupting their studies just when they are gaining most from them, they prejudice their future prospects of promotion and in the short term they have the problems of finding a job.

This is a difficult problem to resolve once it has arisen: the best approach is to prevent it by avoiding the causes, as far as possible.

The difficulty often arises from considering work and school as two totally incompatible alternatives, regarding study as the only thing a student should do, while forgetting the educational and practical benefits of somehow combining a job with school or college (see Chapter 15). Why we put forward this view is the teenager's desire for independence and status; he feels uneasy at having to depend on his parents for money. Hence many feel that they want to go to work at the earliest possible moment simply to earn money on their own account. A short-term job is the best way to gain independence. The influence of friends who already have jobs may be decisive: they can afford expensive things and entertainments, they have a higher standing with members of the opposite sex, they are not a burden on their families and often they are more highly regarded even by their parents. The result is that students feel envious because, not only are they at a financial disadvantage and of lower "standing" than their working friends, but they are still subject to the same continuous pressure as before from parents and teachers with regard to their studies. Besides, they see that some of their friends are no better qualified than they are, and this leads them to the conclusion that success in life does not depend on further education.

In the decision to leave school, the negative influence of the environment also plays a major part. For example, they see adults constantly obsessed with earning and spending money and continually creating new needs for themselves. In a "consumer climate" the youngster "needs" more money and often finds that his pocket-money is insufficient.

Failure at school also tends to play a part in this problem. If a pupil fails his examinations or tests regularly, he feels that they are interminable and then he is reprimanded after each one; in some cases he is even punished by having his pocket-money or free time cut down.

The atmosphere in the school may also tempt pupils to give up school education, if it is not very stimulating or understanding. On this point it must be said that schools are often incapable of satisfying the basic needs of their pupils; for instance, some are geared to deal with the brighter students who have few problems of any kind, and may be less suitable for those who, though not subnormal, have some special difficulties: disinterest in particular subjects, inability to get into the habit of studying etc.

What advice can one give parents to help them prevent this problem? In so far as it is caused by failure at school, our comments on the matter of poor performance are applicable. On another level, they should show a positive attitude to their teenage child's studies — for example, by recognizing the effort he is making, treating it as work rather than as some kind of privilege. They should also avoid exaggerating the "sacrifices we are making" so that the child can stay at school. In poorer families it is not uncommon to "encourage" children by telling them that their parents never had the opportunities or the chances that they are enjoying, that they should do better than their parents etc., expecting — indeed demanding — that the children should constantly feel grateful and — naturally — do well in all their subjects. If they should ever fail an examination, a family drama ensues. Older brothers and sisters not infrequently play a leading role in such dramas if they left school at the earliest possible moment and are now working. They may accuse the student of being a time-waster if he gets a poor result. Such attitudes obviously run the risk of depressing children, or making them feel guilty, and this may push them into looking for a job at the first possible moment.

The family should not confine itself to showing understanding and encouraging the children at home: parents should also try to influence the teachers to do their best at school; they should ensure that the teachers are aware of their children's needs and difficulties, that they have some plan to help and guide them and that they realize that an adolescent cannot be treated or expected to behave in the same way as a primary school child.*

Let us end by mentioning two further measures which may help to prevent this problem: teaching children how to use money properly, and combining study with a job (see Chapter 15). A good grounding in matters relating to money should help teenagers to avoid creating needs for themselves and worshipping money, while a combination of work and study can eliminate many of the cases of leaving school before it is advisable.

*This point deserves fuller treatment than we can devote to it here, because it touches on a common and very important problem, namely that sometimes the only difference between the various levels of education is that the subjects or the syllabuses change, whereas the teachers make no effort to adapt to the changes in the pupil's personality. It is not sufficient to gear the teaching to the "normal" or "typical" psychological needs of the group: each pupil should be known and guided individually.

12

Choosing a career

1. Dangers and consequences of a wrong choice To some extent, all youngsters in the later years of adolescence begin to think about their future and to feel uncertain and anxious with regard to what it may hold. Besides this worry, they also feel a need: the need to be prepared to take their place in the adult world as soon as possible. Having opted for autonomy — to some degree, at least — they need to know what are the chances of being able to achieve it.

This worry and this need explain why the choice of a career is of vital interest to them. It is, in fact, the first time they have had to take a personal stance on one of the most important matters for any person, namely his work or occupation. When we consider that this highly personal decision is taken just in the middle of the growing up process, it is easy to see how important it is for parents and teachers to give it serious attention.

Merely being concerned or even anxious about their future is no guarantee in itself that teenagers will make the right decision. All too often they choose a career or a job for the wrong reasons. One such reason, which is not at all infrequent, is the glamour attached to some professions: they are chosen simply because they are "smart" and have a high social status. In other cases the choice is made purely on the basis of financial considerations.

These superficial (and consequently wrong) decisions can be usually traced back to the harmful influence of parents and friends. Parents sometimes force children into one choice rather than another because, in their view, it is the best; they think that because the children are not yet capable of making wise decisions, they should make them for them. This kind of influence may range from simply raising objections to openly opposing what the children themselves want to do. In fact, it is not unusual for the pressure to be based on one or both of these two considerations, namely income and family tradition. Apart from these potential difficulties or obstacles posed by the family, there are also others: undue eagerness to earn money, changes of interest, the influence of today's comfort-seeking consumer society and the great variety of careers from which to choose.

Young people often tend to make hasty decisions, with little understanding of their own abilities, the opportunities available or the work involved. Their decision may also be based on the temptation to earn money quickly through some lucrative employment. The great range of jobs and types of work potentially available nowadays makes the decision all the more difficult because it becomes essential to know something about what they involve and how far they might suit the aptitudes of each individual.

With so many considerations and influences, obviously any teenager may make a mistake in choosing a career. It would not be an exaggeration to say that without some careers guidance of a psychological and educational type, any choice of job or occupation nowadays can be nothing but a game of chance in which the right decision will be a question of sheer luck. The consequences of making a wrong decision in this important matter are only too well known: failure in examinations or in one's career, feelings of frustration or insecurity, family and social maladjustment. A good illustration of this point is that in Spain, where university entrance is open to very large numbers of students, only 40 per cent of the students who register ever take a degree.

A person's job is so important in his life that it is easy to understand how success or failure can affect his self-confidence. Neither is it difficult to see that if a person is unhappy in his work, he will project his problem on to his home and social surroundings.

A mistake in one's choice of career not only affects the individual himself: it also has repercussions, and very serious ones, on the society to which he belongs. Anyone doing a job which does not suit his talents or interests is bound to under-perform, and yet he makes it impossible for another more suitable person to occupy his post. Thus performance and productivity decrease, with detrimental social consequences.

2. Career guidance   Having pointed to some obstacles that make it difficult for teenagers to choose a career wisely, and given the superficial reasons behind many of the decisions made at this age, one can easily understand the need for proper career guidance. The importance of this was not so obvious in the past, when peoples' occupations were determined more clearly. "In practice, several external circumstances — one's family and social background —

decided the individual's particular occupation: one was born a jeweller, an artisan, a farmer, an aristocrat . . . . Only geniuses and rebels dared to break with the family stability and tradition. The problem of choosing work did not arise" (F. Gallego).[59]

One of the features of our own times, on the other hand, is a remarkable degree of social mobility, and this is reflected in the question of work. It is seen, for instance, in how occupations have changed, the degree of specialization there is, the emergence of new jobs and professions and the promotion available. Undoubtedly these changes have great advantages for the worker in that he can now choose a career, he has far more options open to him, he can change employment or get promotion more easily than before. Nevertheless, the very fact of having to choose, and having the opportunity to do so, gives rise to new problems which can be resolved, especially at such an early age, only with the help of professional advice.

Career guidance makes it possible to suggest to everyone a job to suit his or her aptitudes and interests. The object is, on the one hand, to help each person to know his own talents and limitations and, on the other, to help him understand what is involved and required by the various types of work and to choose the one that best suits him personally. Career guidance is a whole process: it goes on over a period of time. It should be carried out continuously and systematically for each individual, concentrating on his particular characteristics and taking account of the personal and educational performance of his pre-adolescent years.

On this point it is essential to achieve a triple harmony between a number of variables: firstly, between the individual's aptitudes and interests; secondly, between the level of his aspirations and his personal capabilities; thirdly, between the choice he makes and the possibilities of studying or obtaining employment. The point, therefore, is that the decision to be recommended should be the one which the individual will find most useful and interesting, that it should be neither above nor below his capabilities and that the advice should not be given in the abstract but taking the family and social circumstances into account — basically, the family's financial situation and the job market.

Unless the career guidance given to young people fulfils these requirements, it is unlikely to be any real help. For instance, if it is carried out in the space of a few days or if it is confined to administering a few tests, without establishing a genuine personal relationship or taking previous education and upbringing into account, then it is inadequate.

3. Guidelines If we are to encourage career guidance for adolescents along these lines, we must first be clear about who is to carry it out. Since parents are primarily and principally in charge of their children's upbringing, and no one can replace them in this role, it follows that when it comes to giving advice on a career (as on all personal and educational matters) the prime responsibility is still theirs. "The duty and responsibility of guidance belongs to the parents; others may play a part to the extent to which the family is unable to fulfil this grave responsibility"(García Hoz).[60]

Everyone understands that there is no contradiction between remaining primarily responsible for this task and delegating certain aspects of its fulfilment to others. However, on no account should career guidance be left entirely in the hands of teachers or specialists because, like any other part of the children's education, parents have an important role to play in it. They must ensure that such guidance is given and that it is sound; they should keep closely in touch with it throughout the process.

It is therefore a joint undertaking, in which the primary responsibility rests with the parents; the psychologist and the school can help from the technical point of view, but the child himself is, of course, at the centre of the whole process. The fact that career guidance is normally given during adolescence and youth — periods of personality crises and instability — means that the parents' role is all the more decisive and essential. They are in a better position than anyone else to know their child and his needs, and the bonds of affection that unite them with him allow them to help him in a special way. In any case, whether parents are conscious of their role or not, whether they are willing to guide their children or not, the choice of a career always has repercussions on the family which should be foreseen as far as possible.

Apart from this basic responsibility, parents also have a more specific part to play in their child's choice of a career; this can be summarized in two points: first, to cooperate with the teachers and advisers involved and, second, to respect the child's freedom of choice.

On the first point, parents should provide the teachers with details about their child from the beginning of his school life. Contact between the family and the school should be such as to allow and facilitate exchanges of information, so as to ensure that the abilities, limitations and interests of each child are known and kept under review. At parent-teacher interviews, the causes of each particular school performance should be discussed, as well as the likes, dislikes and abilities which the child has shown and any possibilities that may arise in the future etc. In this way the process of career guidance will be linked and integrated into the whole educational process so that, when the time comes to take a decision, parents and teachers will have sufficient information and a sound basis to advise him objectively and realistically, by mutual agreement and without being superficial or over-hasty.

Parents may also play a part by contributing to the information available to all the children in the school. For example, they may cooperate by giving talks to the pupils about their own occupation: the work involved, the aptitudes required, etc.

With regard to the second point, namely respect for the child's freedom of choice, the important thing is to avoid doing or saying anything that would bring pressure to bear on him or coerce him in making his choice. Parents should beware of the danger of projecting themselves on to the child and they must respect his freedom even when they see how immature and inexperienced he is. There are two main reasons for this: first if he has been given some career guidance, then he is not deciding blindly or in the dark, but on the basis of his knowledge of his own capabilities and, second, although if the decision could be taken at a more mature age it would undoubtedly be more likely to be the right one, nevertheless it has to be taken at this stage and therefore a certain risk is inevitable. Besides, career guidance makes sense only in so far as the persons concerned — precisely because of their immaturity and inexperience — have need of it.

Respect for the child's freedom is not based exclusively, however, on purely practical considerations, for there are also more substantial reasons of principle in its favour. Perhaps the most obvious consideration is that everyone has a right to decide freely concerning his own future, and we know that one of the most fundamental aspects of this is his work. Besides, no one can exercise personal responsibility if he has been deprived of the freedom to make a decision.

The duty of parents towards their teenage child with regard to career guidance is to put him in touch with experts, providing him with information, giving him advice and encouraging him to think for himself. In no circumstances, however, should they attempt to think for the child. This requires great unselfishness, seeking only the welfare and happiness of the child, and not the satisfaction of their own pride or particular interests.

On this last point, two questions may be asked: first, how harmful can the influence of the parents' own occupations be on the child's choice and, second, should family interests always and in every case be sacrificed to the child's freedom?

In answer to the first question, we would say that the influence of the parents' work may be dangerous if it has conditioned the child, especially if he has had no opportunity of getting to know other types of occupation. Otherwise, the influence may be quite positive and useful because, as well as being yet another piece of essential information on careers, it can help to create a good atmosphere in which aptitudes and interests, lying latent in the individual, can be developed.

On the second question, we would say that it is better to sacrifice the "family interests" than to sacrifice the legitimate freedom of any member of the family; if the fulfilment of the individual is subordinated to the convenience of the family, the family will cease to exist. The fact that the parents may appease their own temporary frustration is no excuse for running the risk of frustrating the child's whole life.

It is clear, then, that the child must be at the centre of all career guidance, and not the parents or the rest of the family. It is the child who has to decide his own future and it is he who has to take responsibility for his decision.

13

Free time

1. What is free time?   Normally by "free time" we mean time which we can use with a certain amount of discretion, in other words, not connected with our work, with any duty or necessity. The expression also frequently used as equivalent to "leisure", although in fact they are two different, but not unrelated, notions. Speaking of the Latin concept of *otium*, for instance, Cicero considered that it had to consist of activities that were voluntary, creative and pleasant. A sociologist of our own time, Duzamedier, defines leisure as "all the activities to which the individual may devote himself voluntarily, whether to rest or to enjoy himself, to increase his knowledge or to develop his non-professional education, his voluntary participation in social affairs or his free creative abilities, when he has finished his social, family and occupational duties."[61]

Leisure refers, therefore, to "free" occupations connected with the life of the spirit. By "free" we mean, both that they are carried on during our free time, that is, time remaining after our normal duties of various kinds have been fulfilled, and that they are freely chosen and carried out. Leisure is the opposite of any occupation that directly pursues material profit or benefit: etymologically *nec-otium*, non-leisure, gives "negotiation" in the sense of business. Having no pretensions to practical usefulness, leisure seeks only enjoyment through the exercise of some activity.

It follows from what we have said that not everything done outside of one's work and family duties, in other words, during one's free time, can be called a leisure activity. To qualify as leisure, its purpose must be one of the following: relaxation or rest, entertainment or cultural development, exercise of some creative ability or social intercourse. Such activities must be carried out freely by the individual; it is not simply that they may be exercised without any pressure or obligation imposed by others: they also require a certain personal involvement, such as choice and decision. Free time is best understood by contrasting it with the concept of work, which may be understood as onerous, disciplined activity, pursuing some objective, whereas free time activities are more pleasant, require less effort and leave more scope to choose and decide what one wishes to do.

It must be stressed that free time activities also require a certain effort on the part of the individual in so far as they have some objective in view. "There is no clear dichotomy between work and free time, for both are associated with the attitude of making an effort. In a way, the effort expended in pleasant activity is a preparation for that required later in not so pleasant activities" (Isaacs).[62] The difference between work and free time consists in being able to choose what one wants to do, rather than in the amount of effort involved.

The meaning of "free time" has evolved significantly in the course of history. In Greece it had a clearly positive sense; according to Aristotle, for instance, we work in order to have *skolé*, leisure, that is, to be able to devote ourselves freely to occupations which we like, involving the development and exercise of the spirit.[63] The importance attached to utilitarian values at the beginning of the modern era was the reason why leisure came to be regarded as something negative, something "otiose" or idle, useless and lazy, simply a means to replenish our strength to do more arduous work afterwards. Nowadays once again free time activities or leisure have positive connotations. We are more fully aware that life is not all work, that the human being cannot be reduced to being a mere "worker": he works *for* something that goes beyond the actual work itself.

We are witnessing today a development which should not be ignored, namely an increase in the amount of free time available, due to various factors: rationalization of work, automation and the improved social conditions which working people have won for themselves, to name but a few. The five-day-week is now quite normal and there is every indication that we are moving towards a society with more leisure potential and, consequently, with a more human side to it.

2. Education and leisure   Since free time is essential for rest and for the development of the personality, as we have seen, we should not only be aware of what it is but also be ready to use it, and use it properly whenever we have the opportunity — in other words, sensibly, rationally and responsibly. This will not be easy unless we have been properly educated to do so; otherwise free time means nothing but idleness, inactivity and boredom.

Education for leisure should commence at the earliest possible moment and it is the responsibility of the family, schools, employers and society in general. Basically it consists of teaching children and young people to take advantage of the potential benefits of their free time, while avoiding its dangers. Free time is a constant source of knowledge and experience; hence so much insistence on the need to coordinate the influence of the pupils' formal education with less formal effects of the family, the area in which they live, the street, their friends, the press, cinema and television . . . .

This proposed branch of education is hindered by one major obstacle, namely that the people who should put it into practice have not themselves been taught to use their free time properly. This is why, for many parents, leisure is of no value, and why some of them — not to mention some schools — still punish children by depriving them of their free time. It also explains why many adults use their free time unintelligently, thus exercising a decisive influence on youngsters in their attitude to it.

Among the wrong ways in which adults approach this subject, we might mention, first of all, what is sometimes called "workaholism"; this is the vice of people who finish their day's work and then carry on working out of pure inertia, personal vanity or satisfaction, or as an excuse to evade other aspects of their life: family and social duties, for instance. Neither is it uncommon for some people to use work as a drug to save them from having to think or assume certain kinds of responsibility. Other ways of using free time wrongly are to accept passively entertainments "imposed" by others (watching television or playing cards, for instance), to have hobbies that are totally absorbing or to have no hobbies at all.

3. Free time for teenagers   There is no period in our lives when the subject of free time is not relevant, because it is a constant need. Nevertheless during adolescence it is of special importance because of the influence its use may have on the process of developing the young person's personality and his social adjustment: "Leisure-time activities allow the adolescent to be 'at his own disposal' and to take control of his own freedom, allowing him to become autonomous all the more rapidly" (Monera).[64]

The process of change which the teenager undergoes, as we have seen, together with the fact that at this stage a greater effort is required of him than before, whether he continues his studies or takes up a job, sometimes produces conflict, tension and frustration which show how essential it is to have some rest, relaxation and social life. It must also be stressed that the interests that occupy his free time now undergo a very significant change in comparison with middle and later childhood. Childish games are replaced by different activities, such as dancing, watching sports, going to the cinema or driving. "Informal" activities practically disappear and are replaced by more formal ones: for instance, the youngster arranges with his friends to meet at a certain time to play a game with a particular team. Among the activities which are most popular nowadays are sport, outings, various hobbies, dancing, reading, the radio, cinema and television.

Boys are normally more interested in sports and they usually prefer competitive games to the individual type. Outings provide an opportunity to go away from home for a while, to see new situations and places, camping in the open air, fishing or visiting other countries. Teenagers tend to prefer trips where they are not forced to follow any particular routine or be supervised by adults (hitch-hiking has become fashionable both for financial reasons and because of a liking for "non-conventional" journeys). Such trips are of interest at this age only if made with some friends.

Another hobby which many adolescents like is collecting things. Children also collect things, of course, but unlike the child, who keeps everything he can lay his hands on, the teenager is discriminating and collects objects related to his own interests. Again, unlike the child, he does not simply gather things and then forget about them; on the contrary, he enjoys looking after them and showing them to his friends.

As a general rule, dancing appeals to girls more than boys, and they also begin to go to dances at an earlier age. Teenagers are ready to dance anywhere, but they prefer to do so on a good floor, with good music, in a disco or in a hall hired for one of their famous parties.

Reading can become an absorbing interest between the age of twelve and fifteen; at this age youngsters read everything they can get; later on, they begin to concentrate on certain topics. Girls tend to read more than boys and are interested in different subjects. Favourite topics for boys' reading tend to be mysteries, adventure-stories, sports tales, humour, biographies, history, mechanics and travel-stories; girls prefer romantic novels or love-stories, historical novels, fiction and poetry. It is noticeable that newspapers and magazines are of greater interest to youngsters than books and they devote more time to them. There are various reasons for this, such as the following: magazines and newspapers give more up-to-date information, they are read more quickly, cost less and have more varied content than books. A particular section in the newspapers that attracts the attention of these readers is the comic strips; among the many reasons for this, three are particularly relevant: interest in humorous subjects at this age, a liking for the social criticism that often appears in this section and the potential to satisfy certain desires.

Films are one of the favourite pastimes of teenagers. Boys prefer adventure films, thrillers, comedies, warfilms, historical films, westerns, and gangster films, while girls are more attracted to romantic and social themes. Films are usually chosen on the recommendation of friends and normally the main characters tend to be more important than the plot. They go to the cinema in groups and the effect on them is very varied and very deep, as we shall see.

Nowadays the radio is a great attraction for teenagers, mainly because transistors are so readily available. Many keep the radio turned on at all times of the day and night, even when they are studying. Their favourite programmes cover the same subjects as those mentioned with regard to reading material and exercise a profound influence on their attitudes. Their interest in the radio at this age may be attributed basically to the fact that youngsters want to avoid being left alone at any cost; but still feel the need to have someone or something with them all the time.

However, the great monopolizer of an enormous amount of teenagers' free time, and with the harmful effects which we shall mention shortly, is television. This is due more to social circumstances than to their typical likes and dislikes, as we shall also see.

Two important points worth mentioning on this subject are the following: the amount of free time actually decreases in adolescence and the activities that occupy it tend to be fewer in number than previously. The amount of free time is less than before whether the teenager is a student or working; in the former case, he is faced with broader and more complex subjects than at primary school and consequently he has to study more. In the latter case, he often finds that the day's work requires far more effort and concentration than was necessary in previous years. The reduction in the number of activities that occupy his free time results from four main factors, namely the fact that the free time itself is less, as we have just mentioned; the few opportunities offered by the environment, the financial restrictions from which most young people suffer; and their more specialized interests at this age in comparison with childhood.

4. Teenagers' use of their free time   In a survey carried out in Spain among 794 pupils of both sexes, aged between fourteen and seventeen years of age, some quite revealing data were obtained on the subject of their free time. First of all, the actual amount of free time they have is significantly less than people think. "35% of boys and 50% of girls in secondary education have only one free hour or less per day. They complain of having insufficient time; they think this is very little" (Monera, 188). Among the causes of this problem, three in particular are quoted: a heavy school timetable, too much homework and poor methods of working.

Another factor to emerge was the remarkable lack of common sense in their use of whatever free time they had. Thus, for example, there was a notable lack of hobbies, a passive attitude towards environmental influences (films and television especially), no valid criteria for selecting films or reading material, no real critical sense in watching television programmes and films, reluctance to take part in artistic and cultural activities, a preference for organized sports rather than other forms of exercise like walks or trips to the country and over-indulgence in commercialized entertainment.

Despite these findings, "the pupils interviewed claimed to be satisfied with their use of their own free time, saying that by and large they took full advantage of it and were seldom bored" (Monera, 15). They complained of not having suitable places for leisure, of the disinterest shown by grown-ups in what they do in their spare time and of the financial dependence on their parents, having few opportunities to finance their own entertainment.

Furthermore, they rejected any attempt on the part of parents to dictate their free-time activities while, on the other hand, they willingly accepted advice from their friends. They also preferred informal leisure activities to the more organized type. Another very revealing fact was that parents hardly ever supervised their children's use of free time; they were concerned merely to ensure that they avoided certain excesses, but had little interest or knowledge of what they actually did.

5. Problems connected with the use of free time   We have referred to three serious problems which emerged from the survey quoted: insufficient free time, little common sense in its use and inadequate environmental facilities for suitable activities. It may be worth considering the second of these problems here in somewhat more detail.

The lack of common sense in the use teenagers make of their free time is seen in three ways: few formative or educational activities (hobbies, artistic, cultural or social pursuits), too many harmful activities (over-indulgence in commercialized entertainment, harmful reading etc.) and wrong attitudes (passive acceptance of the ways of spending time which are "packaged" and presented in one's environment, little individual thought or critical sense in choosing and carrying out one's activities, lack of effort etc.).

Unsuitable activities during one's free time create bad habits at any age, but especially in adolescence mainly because teenagers are less willing to make an effort than previously. Among such bad habits, laziness and untidiness come to mind, and they tend to get worse during the holidays if these are seen as periods of complete idleness, a non-stop search for nothing but pleasure and the avoidance of any effort. Another consequence of these attitudes is downright boredom, and adolescents are more susceptible to boredom than children for two main reasons, namely they are less curious and need more novelty. Boredom, in turn, tends to give rise to destructive activities in an attempt to compensate for the lack of novelty in their habitual occupations.

Over-indulgence in commercialized entertainment has serious effects on adolescents; for example, they spend too much money (and consequently they have to find it by one means or another), their morals are endangered (due to the harmful atmosphere of certain places: discos, night-clubs etc.); they become "just one of the crowd" and begin to idolise film-stars or sports personalities.

The most harmful free-time activities tend to be connected with the mass media (the press, cinema, radio and television). Alongside the immense educational potential (which teenagers should be taught to discover and use for their own benefit), the media often encourage everyone to think and to act alike, they propagate mental childishness (a willingness to accept only pleasant things) and they discourage reflection (so that people accept the opinions of others passively, without thinking for themselves).

6. Guidelines In teaching adolescents to make proper use of their time, the first thing is to be clear as to what attitudes we wish to instill in them so that they can benefit from the educational advantages free time offers them and avoid the dangers we have just mentioned. The attitudes we have in mind are mainly the following:

— They should always be busy in some activity with an object in view; they should never be idle;

— Whatever they do in their spare time should be done properly, that is to say it should be done to the best of their ability; effortlessness and "letting themselves go" should be avoided, as should the danger of having a dual set of morals: one for work and one for free time.

— They should use their imagination, initiative and individuality in choosing activities, so that these may be varied, kept up to date and connected with each person's interests; this will help them to avoid both the problem of boredom and routine occupations more or less imposed on them by others.

— They should develop a critical sense and personal judgment so as to distinguish activities beneficial to their education from those that may be harmfiul.

To encourage these attitudes in their children, parents must obviously be concerned with the question of their free time. They should ask themselves what they do with their own free time: whether they have any, how highly they value it and how they use it. If they unthinkingly adopt the activities imposed by the lifestyle of the area in which they live, they will scarcely be in a position to encourage any better attitudes in their children. The same applies to those who are "workaholics", suffer from boredom or have no hobbies.

The value that we attach to our own free time should be in proportion to the importance we give to that of others. In this regard it is essential to respect our children's free time (by not insisting, for example, that they study or help in the house all the time). This outlook on the part of parents will help children to discover the importance of free time for their own development and will encourage them to find it, even though, as we have seen, it is harder to find than it was when they were younger. Concern for children's leisure should be exercised according to certain rules:

1. Parents should teach them to choose activities and should make suggestions for things to do, but always respecting their own personal likes and dislikes.

2. They should, somehow or other, keep a check on how the children use their free time, either directly or indirectly; they should always know where they are, what they are doing and how they are doing it; one constructive suggestion, for instance, would be for parents and children to spend and enjoy some of their free time together.

3. They should plan some activities with their children, having

specific aims in view; such plans, however, and the supervision of their implementation should not stop the children from having plenty of opportunity to occupy themselves also in unorganized, less formal ways.

4. They should try to achieve a balance between the time devoted to work and to rest, taking account of each individual's circumstances: age, school performance etc.

5. Children should be given an opportunity to play a part in the family chores; for instance, by assigning them jobs in the house on a rotating basis.

6. During their free time they should be given an opportunity to have a job, apart from their studies (see Chapter 15).

7. They should be required to put effort into everything they undertake and to finish it properly; they should be encouraged to do a few things well rather than many things badly.

8. A check should be kept on the amount of money they have and they should be taught to use it properly. The virtue of moderation is very important for teenagers nowadays: the dangers of commercialized entertainment and over-spending are ever-present (see Chapter 14).

9. They should be encouraged to undertake open-air activities whenever possible: outings, walks, camping etc.

10. Some permanent form of collaboration should be established with the school to coordinate the children's free-time activities, especially during the holidays.

Parents should also keep in mind some basic notions relating in particular to three favourite occupations of teenagers in their free time, namely reading, films and television.

With regard to the first point, parents should always know what kind of books, magazines etc. their children are reading. There is always the danger that they may get their hands on harmful publications; for instance, material containing errors of religious doctrine, propagating ideologies of a totalitarian type or attacking morals. This requires that parents should be sufficiently well informed to be able to distinguish what is good from what is harmful to their children. The sensible and wise thing would be to seek advice from someone scientifically and morally qualified to give guidance on what the children are reading and what they should read in the future. They should certainly be encouraged to enjoy reading, but always ensuring that they do so with sound critical sense and judgment. This will come about provided parents do not confine themselves to forbidding harmful books, but also explain exactly their reasons for doing so in each particular case.

With regard to films, one objective to be aimed at is that children should learn to choose what they want to see on sound principles of their own. For example, it would be foolish to go to a particular cinema just because their friends are going, because the latest film is being shown, because it has some well known film star or it is near home. Their decision should be based on artistic and moral criteria, and this involves being sufficiently interested to obtain information in advance: by asking somebody whose opinion can be trusted, reading the film critics, noting its certificate. . . . Parents should provide their children with this kind of information and give them ideas on how to judge the film both before and after seeing it. With this in mind, it is a good idea for the whole family to discuss the films seen by the children; it will help too if parents go with them now and then.

On the subject of television, the time allowed for sitting in front of the small screen should be strictly limited. This can be achieved if children are taught to select their viewing according to some principle. As in the case of films, some information about the content of the various programmes will be required but nowadays this is not difficult: newspapers and magazines contain advance information of this kind. Another point is children should not adopt a purely passive attitude to all the "messages" disseminated by television; it is essential to encourage some personal thought and critical capacity, and this can be achieved by teaching them to distinguish what is real from what is fictitious, facts from opinions, the artistically and morally good from the bad etc. These important distinctions can be clarified after each television programme if the family gets into the habit of commenting on what they have seen.

14

Use of money

1. Financial problems The problems that may arise in connection with the use of money during adolescence usually derive from two facts: first, teenagers need more money than children, not only because they are older but because they often create needs for themselves; and, second, they want to have money of their own to use as they think best.

On this basis, a kind of dilemma frequently arises: on the one hand, teenagers are seldom satisfied with the pocket-money they receive from their parents while, on the other hand, they feel uncomfortable at having to depend on them for all their expenses. Their anxiousness to have more money of their own is the reason why so many teenagers try to get a job as soon as they can and consequently, in some cases, leave school at the first possible moment, as mentioned in the previous chapter. Obviously a desire to work is not in itself wrong or something to be discouraged. It is only inadvisable if the youngsters have the aptitude and the opportunity to continue studying, and give up school simply to earn money of their own.

These attitudes are greatly intensified by certain influences of the consumer society in which we live: the "need" to maintain a certain rate of production leads to increased pressure by means of advertising to get consumers to consume more and then to find new customers for new products. This increases the desire to spend more, instead of spending more wisely. In this consumer atmosphere teenagers have become a very important sector of the market.

The example of grown-ups, and especially of their parents, is another important factor in the development of these consumer attitudes on the part of adolescents. Adults not infrequently treat money as an end in itself: "Money is desired because it gives a certain status, because it means power or because it compensates for some kind of shortcoming or failure. Not having money is regarded as a great misfortune; it is spoken about very bitterly; it becomes incompatible with having a sense of humour." (Otero)[66]

It is easy to see why an atmosphere in which people try to earn money at any cost (often at the expense of others), and to earn it simply to spend it again (as a result of continually creating new needs), should be a fertile breeding ground for more and more teenagers' whims and wants. The desire to have money of their own as a means towards greater independence, together with the influences of such an environment, may cause teenagers to worship money. Here a significant role is also played by the need to communicate with their peers by different methods from those of earlier ages: buying certain objects such as clothes, records, magazines etc., simply as a means of contact between them. When we remember that today's adolescents also have more money than their predecessors, we realize what an easy life many of them lead, spending large sums of money in a totally superfluous and unnecessary manner.

Consequently the teenager of today has little interest in saving money; on the one hand, he seldom has much left over to save while, on the other, saving is not highly regarded among youngsters and could lower their "standing". Some try to excuse their failure to save by pointing to inflation and the depreciation in the value of money. They say it is better to be in debt than to have money saved, an argument with which many adults agree — and perhaps they are not altogether wrong.

It is remarkable that sometimes teenagers worship money and despise it at the same time. This is basically due to two factors: their own idealism and the influence of grown-ups. Their idealism makes them despise everything material and oppose the bourgeois lifestyle that comes from the possession of wealth. (One expression of this is the bohemian way of life adopted by some young people.) Their idealism is intensified if they see adults who also have contempt for wealth and the wealthy. This worship of money and contempt for it at the same time is a kind of contradiction which seems incomprehensible; for instance, in some teenagers who never wear anything but casual clothes (jeans, for example) and dress very informally, but yet pay more for such "gear", very often, than they would for "elegant" adult clothes.

2. Guidelines It is surprising that, on a question such as this, where both children and parents are constantly making decisions, there is virtually no established system of guidance. This is all the more astonishing when we consider the potential that the use of money has for the development of certain human qualities: sense of responsibility, moderation and generosity, in particular. Since there is no specific educational method on the correct use of money, it means that children and grown-ups carry on without any set principles, in many cases allowing themselves to be carried along passively by personal whims and the influence of the consumer society.

All the more reason, therefore, for parents to be aware of the vital importance the right and wrong use of money may have for their children and to take another look at their own attitudes to the subject. Although the main problems related to the correct use of money arise in adolescence, education on this matter should begin much earlier. Unless children learn to behave responsibly and moderately at an early age, they will have difficulty in overcoming the dangers that emerge later on.

It is therefore important for children to learn little by little to administer their pocket-money, spending only whatever is necessary, buying something useful, getting used to saving, waiting for the right time to buy whatever they need . . . . In this way they will acquire habits of self-control and moderation.

Handling money can also teach them to be generous. This will involve getting them accustomed to sharing whatever they have with others who may be in need. They could be asked to save a small sum for charity and the apostolate, the missions, for instance, and to make some contribution to the family expenses: the actual account may be very small — it is the symbolic value that matters.

If these goals are to be attained, it is imperative that the home atmosphere should discourage superfluous spending, that financial difficulties should never become a permanent source of frustration and that the parents should be able to say no to the whims of their children. One possible arrangement is to assign a certain allowance as pocket-money on a regular basis, depending on the child's age, so that he will learn to use it responsibly. This will entail observing how he behaves and correcting him whenever necessary and it will only work provided no exceptions are made: the allowance must not vary from week to week and it must not be paid out before it is due.

The amount will depend on the circumstances: the child's age, the financial position of the family, etc. No figure can therefore be suggested here; the point is that it should be neither more nor less than the child needs for his own reasonable expenses. If there is an atmosphere of mutual trust in the family, everyone will be able to discuss the matter freely: the children will put in their "applications" and the parents will feel free to grant or refuse them.

Something to avoid is giving or taking money as a reward or a punishment, for this would encourage an unhealthy love of it.

In training adolescents to manage their finances properly, there appear to be three basic problems:

1. A desire for money as a response to an immediate eagerness for independence;

2. Over-spending or mis-spending, and

3. The influence of the consumer society, especially through advertising.

With regard to the first problem, it must be repeated that it is quite normal for youngsters to want to have their own money at this age. But this may be a cause of problems, if earnings provide a means of severing their dependence on their parents; financial independence also tends to bring about a break with parents in other ways. Consequently parents should try to discover what exactly it is within the family atmosphere that is creating this excessive and premature desire for financial self-sufficiency on the part of the children.

Sometimes it may be a reaction to certain parental attitudes or rules. For instance, teenagers find it very unpleasant and humiliating to have to ask for money each time they need it and having to account for how they spend it. They find it even more humiliating if parents give them an account showing how much they have "paid" them, especially if their pocket-money is related to their marks at school, their behaviour or the "sacrifices" made by the parents. In such cases, financial dependence may be seen by children at best as a privilege and, at worst, as a form of oppression. In either case the reaction will be the same: a determination to earn money as soon as possible, even if it means abandoning duties and obligations previously contracted, such as those connected with education.

To prevent this problem, children should have whatever sums of money they need; pennilessness or tight purse-strings may drive them to look for finances in ways that would be bad for themselves and the family. Naturally the allowance will depend both on the family circumstances and what the parents think is reasonable. In any case, parents and children should discuss the matter in a spirit of trust and they could also consider the possibility of combining school with a job that would bring in some income.

It is advisable too for pocket-money to be allocated to teenagers for longer periods than is the case with young children: for instance, even for a month or more. This will help them to see the advantages of working out a budget for their income and expenditure and to keep some kind of account or check on how their money is spent.

With regard to the second problem mentioned above, it must be said that teenagers seldom see any need for self-control in financial matters. Many would regard this as nothing but senseless inhibitions or restrictions especially in the atmosphere of today's consumer society; they tend to say that spending their money as they think best does no harm to anybody. To influence them on this matter they must be made aware that "Each individual should take responsibility for his own life, in such a way as to make good use of everything he possesses, in the service of God, and of others. He must not only avoid doing harm: he must also do positive good. There is no point in spending his money and time simply for his own pleasure; he must use them for his own benefit and the benefit of others." (Isaacs)[67] If adolescents are to accept this approach, they will have to discover that money is not an end in itself, nor even a means to be used directly in the pursuit of pleasure: above these purposes, there is a higher goal.

To guide teenagers on the subject of the third problem mentioned above, namely the influence of the consumer society, the basic point is to help them to acquire valid principles as a basis for correct decisions. David Isaacs proposes four such principles: 1) consideration of the possible repercussions on the youngster's own improvement if he does or does not make a particular purchase; 2) the question of whether spending in a particular way could be regarded as an injustice towards others; 3) consideration of the true motive for making a particular purchase; 4) thought as to whether their behaviour is creating new needs for themselves.[68]

There is no need to emphasize the impact of environment on the achievement of this objective. Moderation should be a constant aim of the whole family, starting with the parents: otherwise, the children will not only have little encouragement to try harder in an area which they already find very difficult, but they will even be tempted to accuse the parents of living in a spendthrift manner while expecting their children to do exactly the opposite.

15

Work

This chapter should more accurately be entitled "Students who work" in order to make it clear from the outset that its purpose is not to deal with young people who have left school or college and are working full time. Obviously, a student's work consists, above all else, of studying. This is undoubtedly a form of human work: intellectual work. A student can therefore be considered as having an occupation like any other worker, namely study.

Certainly study is "work in the field of education"; that is, it is the means and the opportunity of improving oneself on the human and supernatural levels, provided it fulfils certain conditions. These refer not only, and not even primarily, to the activity of studying, but more especially to the way in which it is done. Here we have in mind intellectual work properly done in a spirit of service to others, in the pursuit of a certain objective, carried out in order to develop one's own freedom and that of other people and to make it possible to take personal decisions.

Having clarified this, we may ask ourselves the following question: To what extent is a person (in this case, a normal student) who is engaged exclusively in one form of work (namely study) over a number of years genuinely educating himself? If education is supposed to be preparation for life, how much and what kind of preparation is such a person actually receiving? Of course, it would be very easy at this point to exaggerate all the faults in the educational system — learning mainly from books or only in the classroom, the gap between the curriculum and social change, etc. — but these factors are not essential to the relevance of our question: even if these and other defects in the education system were remedied, the question would still require an answer.

Is it possible to educate a child for life while keeping him out of contact with life? We are so accustomed to the fact that students do nothing but study, we are so used to the system, that these questions may seem strange to us; they are the kind of question that, even if they seem to point to possible improvements, nevertheless they strike us as just one more attempt to complicate things unnecessarily.

The experiment of studying and working simultaneously is still far from common in most countries, although in some, such as the United States, students in high school and at university quite commonly combine study with some form of work, and only in exceptional cases do they study full-time. Those familiar with this know that normally not only are one's studies not prejudiced by part-time work, but they actually improve: in the United States there are many brilliant professionals who "worked their way through college". The worker who studies part-time (a phenomenon which is becoming more and more common out of necessity) is being joined nowadays by the student who works part-time.

The point we wish to bring to the reader's attention has recently been studied by Professor Victor García Hoz and concerns the possibility of education for work alongside the normal education at school or college. Obviously on this issue, as on others, the opinions of parents and teachers are divided and therefore it may be worth while analysing, however briefly, the pros and cons of the matter.

1. Why a student should work   The reasons why a student should also have a job may be clarified, first of all, by setting out some of the dangers of regarding study and work as incompatible alternatives. One such danger is that of the idle student, living at the expense of others — whether his parents or society — and doing nothing to make his situation less burdensome on those others. Parents of teenage pupils, therefore, should try to ensure at any cost that they avoid an "easy life" attitude. Another danger, closely related to this, is that they may not appreciate the value of money; if they have made no effort to earn money, it is not easy to live moderately or to avoid waste and self-indulgence.

A third danger of full-time study is a dramatic increase in the difficulties which adolescents find in adjusting to family life. This is usually the reason why leaving school early arises: they find a job simply to end their financial dependence on the family.

Another reason why a student should also have a job may be explained by the principle that young people should not be deprived of the experience of work done as seriously as someone earning his living would do it. In other words, they should not miss the opportunity of having some responsibility in an area different from their studies, for every line of work has its own potential for exercising such responsibility. Besides, this experience will involve contact with real life, acquiring direct knowledge of the society in which we live, developing new capabilities, training to some extent for a future career, developing an attitude of service of others and discovering the real meaning of study . . . .

Finally, the combination of study and a job makes it easier for children to understand their parents better: they get to know their difficulties, sacrifices and problems. Being able to make a contribution to the family budget and having some money left over for their own expenses also helps to promote a more positive relationship between them and their parents.

2. Dangers and difficulties of the working student   Having seen the advantages, let us see the disadvantages of combining a job with one's studies. We shall refer to the dangers and difficulties pointed out by some parents.

One of the objections put forward is that in the areas where they live, or the circles in which they move, it is not customary for students to have a job, and therefore it creates a bad impression and looks bad: sending a child "out to work" while still at school or college would undoubtedly mean either that the family's financial situation had deteriorated drastically or that the parents were exploiting their children, or both of these things. Parents in this situation allege that, as well as causing comment among their acquaintances, the children would also have a poor opinion of them.

Another difficulty mentioned is of a more practical type, namely that it is far from easy to find jobs for students. Some parents report that they have failed to find even unpaid work for their children. Many employers either have no vacancies or have little confidence in the efficiency or sense of responsibility of students. When they do find a job, it seldom suits their aptitudes and interests.

The third difficulty derives from the fact that the young person himself has to be consulted. Some students object to working, either in general or to some particular type of work. In the former case the reasons may be many: fear of finding themselves in an unfamiliar situation, of taking on new responsibilities, of not being able to cope with two occupations or simply unwillingness to make the effort involved. In the latter case, he may refuse a particular job because it does not suit him.

Besides these difficulties, there are two dangers which must be mentioned, namely that the youngsters may neglect their studies, or even give them up completely, and that the work atmosphere may be harmful. The first of these dangers arises either because the job is more attractive than study or because it is impossible to cope with both and one has to suffer. With regard to the second danger, many reports speak of situations where young people are working closely with grown-ups of both sexes and there is always the danger of harmful influences from the moral point of view.

3. Guidelines How serious is the difficulty of allowing one's children to have a job while still students because it would create a bad impression in the neighbourhood? We might answer: it is only as serious as the parents wish. If they themselves are convinced that this is only a prejudice that should be resisted, even if it means going against the current, then the question has no further importance. The real problem arises when it is the parents themselves who have this prejudice or at least agree with it to some degree. The "life of leisure" student mentality is not something that appears out of nowhere: it has a lot to do with the attitudes and environment of each particular area.

The difficulty of actually finding jobs for students is indeed very real in many cases. Unfortunately, as yet in our society not enough value is attached to work done by anyone who does not fit the standard description: "Young man, 25-30, experience essential". The blame for this should be placed fairly and squarely on the shoulders of those who are depriving society of the benefits of the talents of young men and women and, indeed, are opposing the exercise of a basic human right.

We repeat that the difficulty is a real one, but it is no more than that: a difficulty. Therefore there is no point in just complaining; we should do something practical either to overcome it in each particular case or to see that it disappears or decreases in general. Fortunately, there are some employers who give jobs to students, even if this is motivated by financial considerations, in that unqualified temporary workers are paid less than others. In any case, there is no point in waiting for a job to appear of its own accord: we have to go out and look for it. The child himself should also be involved in the search, so that he will realise that it is his problem.

The suggestion that we have to be out and about if we want to find work is confirmed by many students who have found jobs of various kinds, either during the holidays or throughout the year: doing surveys, distributing leaflets, baby-sitting, delivering bills and letters etc. It would, of course, be ideal if the work found was suited to the long-term aptitudes, interests and even ambitions of the student, but we would suggest that for temporary work this should not be strictly necessary. It will undoubtedly be essential, on the other hand, for one's future career, in other words, for whatever work one does after finishing one's education and training.

What should parents do if a child shows no interest, or even objects to taking a job while still a student? Obviously the first thing is to find out his reasons. After hearing what he has to say, if it appears that his disinterest or objections are based simply on laziness, he should be shown, not only the various advantages for himself of having a job, but also that he has a genuine responsibility — to himself, to others and to God — to do so. We repeat here the goal proposed to parents earlier in this book, namely to avoid an "easy-life" attitude on the part of their children at all costs.

If the youngster's reason for objecting to a job is fear of a new situation, the wisest thing would be to bring him into contact with such a situation little by little, in such a way that neither much time nor much responsibility is involved at the beginning. For example, before accepting a permanent post it would be useful if he had some work experience during holiday periods and, even before that, some familiarity with work without any commitment on his part.

If we have good reason to believe that a child will be unable to cope with both a job and study, the sensible thing will be not to let him embark on any type of work. However, it would not seem right to deprive him categorically and definitely of such experience, for this would involve, as we have said, a serious gap in his education; rather, a job should be found that would require little effort, or it should be offered to him at the right moment etc.

With regard to the danger that the job may be harmful to the child's study, it would seem that the degree of risk involved will depend to a great extent on the attitude of the parents. The risk will increase, for instance, if they ignore certain environmental factors (workmates, spending habits . . .), if they neglect to advise the children on the use of money or if they fail to keep a check on their studies. In any case, there is always some degree of risk which must be taken.

On the question of possible dangers from the work environment, obviously parents should inform themselves on this matter in advance. They can see what the atmosphere is like simply by visiting the workplace, asking people in positions of responsibility and, naturally, by speaking to the child himself. The attitude they should adopt will depend on the circumstances of each particular situation. Sometimes it will be quite sufficient to give the child good advice; in other cases, the only sensible thing would be for him not to accept that particular job.

The guidelines we have suggested here must be seen merely as an approach to the subject: a subject which is of recent origin and requires a lot of thought on the part of parents and teachers because of the impact it can undoubtedly have on children's education.

Summary

In these final pages, it may be useful to present a brief summary of the whole subject outlined in the book. The points that seem most important are the following:

1. No study of adolescence should confine itself to any one phase or stage in the individual's development. The subject is much broader in scope than could be treated within the strict limits of developmental psychology. A study of adolescence implies some understanding of childhood and adulthood. Childhood should be treated as an essential point of reference to approach the subject of adolescence because, depending on each particular case, it may help or hinder the resolution of the crisis to come. Adulthood, on the other hand, is relevant because it is the outcome or end of adolescence and because, in some cases, it is a kind of prolonged adolescence.

Adolescence may therefore be regarded as a focus for an overall study of the various stages and aspects of the education and upbringing of the individual.

2. The basic problem of adolescents has not changed throughout the ages, namely learning to cope on their own and adjusting to new and more difficult situations than they had to deal with in childhood. Yet it is necessary to point this out to parents and teachers because nowadays the problem is more acute than in the past, as a result of a number of social changes which we are witnessing. The fact that society today is in some ways more insecure than in the past seriously hinders the transition from childhood to adulthood. Therefore it is more necessary than before to view the adolescence in the context of the home and social environment in which he really lives, taking account of the influences of all kinds which affect him.

3. Difficulties in parent-child relationships need not be regarded as exceptional; in one form or another, they arise to some extent in

practically every case; they are quite normal and have a valid explanation in the light of certain circumstances. The gap between parents and their teenage children is threefold — biological, psychological and generational — and this in itself explains why communication and understanding between them is bound to be difficult. On the other hand, open or persistent conflict cannot be regarded as anything but anomalous, but this must and can be avoided in most cases if the parents have brought their children up properly, both before and during adolescence. In this regard, we believe that the most decisive factor in the teenager's adjustment to his new situation is precisely the attitude of the parents.

4. The typical immaturity of the adolescent should not necessarily be seen as a backward step in his development. His immaturity becomes evident in his conduct because the adolescent *wants* to exercise his autonomy and act according to his own principles. Immaturity of the type found in childhood and adulthood, on the contrary, takes exactly the opposite form: it is conformist and makes no demands on the person. This should make parents and teachers very aware of the educational potential to be found in many forms of adolescent behaviour.

5. The nature and even the very existence of adolescence depend to a great extent on the social conditions in which an individual lives. In comparison with other periods in the past, the later school-leaving age and longer studies nowadays mean that many teenagers enter the adult world later; consequently their dependence on grown-ups is correspondingly protracted. This involves education advantages but also new problems for parents and teachers. Young people today tend to be more mature in personality than previously but, on the other hand, they reach that maturity later; they are exposed to all kinds of information and they learn a lot but yet they do not benefit, for example, from the experience of short-term or temporary work.

6. While there have always been problems of understanding between the generations, today these are aggravated by the indifference of generations towards one another. This happens because young people are constructing a society of their own, which often is quite separate from adult society. Various factors contribute to this: one of the main causes is the influence of the media, which have put young people in closer contact with one another nowadays, even across national boundaries. Another factor is the lack of stimulus or encouragement

offered to youth by today's adult society. How to break down this indifference and bridge the generation gap is an important challenge for parents and teachers today.

7. Teenage rebellion is a form of protest against the very idea of subordination implied in the notion of obedience. However, we must distinguish the rebellion of youth both from the disobedience of a child and from obstinacy and critical spirit in adolescents. None of these attitudes necessarily involves an open refusal to be subject to grown-ups. The rebellion of young people today is inspired by new motives and poses new problems. For instance, they are often in profound disagreement with the adult world and claim the right to set up a system of their own.

In dealing with this problem an important part is played by the attitudes of the parents and their success or failure in checking the influence of the environment. It is not so much a question of suppressing such rebellious tendencies but rather of directing them towards higher and more positive goals. Essentially, the object is to get the youngsters to opt for a progressive form of rebellion, based on the idea of duty and inspired by love, and to avoid those other forms that are aggressive, retrograde or delinquent.

8. The danger of running away from home has increased considerably in recent years, as has the number of those who never return. These two facts are associated with poor psychological and educational conditions in the home and with the help that teenagers expect and receive nowadays from their "emancipated" friends. In preventing this danger, the climate in the home plays a decisive role. It is very important that the child feel fully integrated within the family and this means that he needs to be satisfied in his basic need to be accepted, to feel secure and to develop his own personality.

9. Although shyness is not something peculiar to adolescence, it tends to be especially noticeable at this stage and stems from lack of confidence in oneself and others. Shyness is more common in adolescents basically for two reasons: the emergence of a new ability to reflect and the need to adjust to an unknown and sometimes unfavourable environment.

Shyness and feelings of inferiority are usually connected, for shyness is simply a consciousness of some weakness. To prevent this problem, we should avoid intolerance, undue severity, and anything that might humiliate and embarrass. Every effort should be made to surround children with an understanding, friendly atmosphere, helping them to develop all their abilities and talents. To overcome their shyness, we should encourage them to accept themselves as they are and to have confidence in their abilities.

10. The danger of doing less well at school than previously should not be attributed to laziness. It arises to a great extent from the physical and mental developments taking place in normal adolescents. They now need new motivation to do their best, and parents and teachers should help them to overcome their new difficulties.

11. The danger of leaving school early is due in some cases to regarding study and work as incompatible alternatives. Another cause sometimes is the feeling that students are enjoying some kind of privilege. This risk will be diminished if parents attach a realistic degree of importance to study, if they teach their children to use money properly and if they regard work and study as compatible activities.

12. Mistakes in choosing a career are usually the result of a hasty decision or of the harmful influence of parents and friends. Youngsters need proper career guidance today more than ever before because of the mobility that now exists in the job market. Career guidance is a long process; it should commence before adolescence and continue side by side with ordinary education.

It is the parents who are primarily responsible for ensuring that their children get good, helpful advice on careers, even though they may rely on teachers and counsellors for certain aspects of it. It is particularly important for them to respect the freedom of their children in their choice of a career, both on principle (respect for the individual) and for more practical reasons.

13. There is no radical difference between work and free time. Both involve the pursuit of some goal and an effort to attain it, through personal effort and making demands on oneself. The difference is that free time activites allow greater freedom of choice, are usually more pleasant and require less effort.

Teenagers should be taught to use their free time properly so as to face up to certain dangers that arise nowadays: passive acceptance of whatever the environment imposes, lack of any critical sense in accepting or rejecting "what everyone does" and disinterest in educational activities.

It is also essential to create more opportunities for teenagers to be involved in suitable activities during their free time, so as to avoid excessive reliance on commercialized entertainment. Parents should somehow or other keep a check on their children's use of free time and this requires, in turn, that they practise what they preach.

14. Problems related to finance arise because teenagers need more money than before and they want to have their own, to spend as they choose. This may lead to the idea of seeking a job as soon as possible, even if it means leaving school early. The problems tend to be aggravated by the influence of the consumer society in which they live, which encourage them to spend more rather than to spend more wisely.

Young people receive scarcely any education on the use of money, which means that they have no rules or principles to guide them. Training in the use of money should commence long before adolescence; children should learn to manage money from a young age and acquire habits of self-control and moderation.

This virtue of moderation is most important in adolescence, precisely because during this phase it is misunderstood and not much admired. Youngsters must be taught that money can and should be used for their own benefit and that of others.

15. Full-time study over a number of years, including the periods of adolescence and youth, is a system which has grave shortcomings with regard to the individual's overall development; nor is it devoid of dangers. It deprives the child of the experience of working as hard as someone who earns his living and shelters him from direct contact with the life and the society to which he belongs. It encourages an "easy life", makes it difficult for the individual to fit into the family atmosphere and realise the true meaning of money.

Despite the difficulties that may arise in trying to combine a job with one's studies, parents should not give up the attempt to get their children to do so, although it may take a different form and be interpreted differently in each particular case.

Notes

1   M. Débesse, *La adolescencia* (Barcelone 1962), *pages* 9 and 21.

2   T. A. Jersild, *Psicología de la adolescencia* (Madrid 1965), 4.

3   B. Del Moral,"Padres y educadores ante la juventud" in *Comunidad educativa* (January 1967), 6, quoted by P. Orive in *Riesgos de la adolescencia* (Madrid 1972) 37.

4   P. Orive, op. cit., quotes facts relating to failure at school, failure to adapt, violence, juvenile delinquency, sexual deviations, drugs and running away from home, among other dangers to which today's adolescents are exposed.

5   M. Yela: *Educación y libertad* (Bilbao, 1967), 71.

6   This point is treated by V. García Hoz, *El nacimiento de la intimidad* (Madrid 1970), 18.

7   *Unos días en la vida de Almudena Hernández:* Case number OF-97, School of Education, University of Navarre, Spain.

8   Cf. G. Cruchon, *Psicología pedagógica*, vol. II (Madrid 1971), 67.

9   OF-97, loc. cit., 8.

10   Cf. *Desarrollo dinámico de la personalidad: pubertad y adolescencia*, Technical note OF-77, School of Education, University of Navarre, 6.

11   Cf. O. F. Otero, "La educación de la libertad y el adolescente" in *Padres y adolescentes*, Pamplona, University of Navarre, 1972, p 47.

12   A. Wallenstein, *La educación del nino y del adolescente* (Barcelona 1967), 203.

13   Cf. A. Schneiders, *Los adolescentes y el reto de la madurez* (Santander 1969), 57 and 58.

14   L. Prohaska, *El procesa de la maduración en el hombre* (Barcelona 1973), 11.

15   M.J. Cantista, *El valor y su fundamentación ontológica*, Technical Note, School of Education, University of Navarre.

16   Ibid.

17   V. García Hoz, *Educación personalizada* (Madrid 1970), 27.

18   R. Guardini, *La aceptación de si mismo* (Madrid 1962), 63.

19   OF-97, loc. cit.

20   J.I. Carrasco de la Paula, "Adolescencia y juventud" in *Gran Enciclopedia Rialp*, vol. II, (Madrid), 242.

21 Plato, *Timaeus* quoted by L. Prohaska, op. cit., 47.

22 See O. Durr, *La obediencia del nino* (Barcelona 1968), 37f.

23 Cf. David Isaacs, *Character building: a guide for parents and teachers* (Dublin 1984), 77-80.

24 See O.F. Otero, *Educación y manipulación* (Pamplona 1975), 64.

25 Cf. Otero, art. cit., 63.

26 See David Isaacs, op. cit., 131.

27 See David Isaacs, op. cit., 115.

28 J. Lacroix, *Timidez y adolescencia* (Barcelona 1974), 26.

29 P. Rodríguez, "Acerca del estilo universitario" in *Nuestro Tiempo*, No. 185 (Pamplona) November 1969, 483.

30 Eduard Spranger, *Psicología de la edad juvenil* (Madrid 1961), 47.

31 V. García Hoz, *La calidad y el derecho a la educación* in *ABC* (Madrid), 22 October 1977.

32 M. J. Hildebrand, "Psicología del aprendizaje y de la ensenanza" quoted in *Diálogo Familia-Colegio*, No. 33 (Granada 1968), 3.

33 See G. Cruchon, op. cit., 360.

34 M.J. Hildebrand, "Juventud nueva" in *Diálogo Familia-Colegio*, no. 33, 5.

35 See P. Laurie, *La rebeldía de la juventud* (Barcelona 1969), 15.

36 See J.J. López Ibor, *Peligro en las aulas* (Madrid 1975), 35.

37 J. Leif and J. Delay, *Psicología y educación del adolescente*, vol. II, (Buenos Aires, 1971), 297.

38 See Leif and Delay, op. cit., 544-546.

39 M. Yela, "Juventud y rebeldía" in *Anuario de los Colegios San Estanislao de Kostka* (1968), 64.

40 See M. Yela, art. cit., 66.

41 See R. Gomez, *Jóvenes rebeldes (temores y esperanzas)* (Madrid 1976), 21.

42 Ibid.

43 G. Bonani *et al.*, *Jóvenes nueva frontera* (Bilbao 1970), 9.

44 J.J. López Ibor, *Rebeldes* (Madrid 1966), 17.

45 J.R. Gallagher and H.I. Harris, *Emotional problems of adolescents* (New York 1976), 43.

46 See J.L. Simancas, *Tres supuestos básicos de la acción tutorial*, Technical note CO-93, School of Education, University of Navarre, 1975.

47 J. Favez-Boutonier, "La educación del adolescente" in *Escuela de Padres y Educadores*, No. 11, (Barcelona 1966), 4, 5.

48 J. Pieper, report of lecture by in *Aceprensa* 173/74 (Madrid) 6 November 1974.

49 R. Mucchielli, *La personalidad del nino* (Barcelona 1969).

50   See Cruchon, op. cit., 181.

51   See Leif and Delay, op. cit., 554.

52   See C.L. Allaer *et al.*, *La adolescencia* (Barcelona 1976), 293.

53   Ibid., 284.

54   Ibid., 286.

55   Ibid., 289.

56   Ibid., 289.

57   *Shyness*, National Film Board of Canada, 106 B-3853-011.

58   Gerardo Castillo, *Metodología del trabajo intelectual y consecuencias para la dirección de un centro educativo*, Technical note CO-117, School of Education, University of Navarre.

59   F. Gallego, "La orientación profesional" in *Padres y adolescentes* (Pamplona 1972), 119.

60   V. García Hoz, *Principos de pedagogía sistemática* (Madrid 1973), 195.

61   Quoted in *Gran Enclicopedia* Rialp, vol XVII (Madrid), 214.

62   David Isaacs, *Re-Unión familiar* (Barcelona, 1974), 68.

63   *Gran Enciclopedia Rialp*, vol XVII, 214.

64   M.L. Monera, "El tiempo libre como elemento de personalización" in *Bordón*, 194-5, February-March 1973, 187.

65   Cf. ibid., 188.

66   O. F. Otero, *El dinero como medio educativo*, Technical note OF-14, School of Education, University of Navarre, 3.

67   David Isaacs, *Character building*, op. cit., 116.

68   Cf. ibid., 117.

OTHER WORKS NOT REFERRED TO ABOVE

Avanzani, G., *Los anos de la adolescencia* (Barcelona 1971).
Baca, E. *et al*, *Padres y adolescentes* (Pamplona 1972).
Castillo, Gerardo, *Sabemos aprender?* (Madrid 1976).
F. Otero, O., *Autonomía y autoridad en la familia* (Pamplona 1975)
Garrigo, A. *La rebeldía universitaria* (Madrid, 1970).
Ginott, H.G. *Entre padres y adolescentes* (Barcelona 1970).
Hurlock, E., *Psicología de al adolescencia* (Buenos Aires 1967).
López Ibor, J.J., *El descubrimiento de la intimidad y otros ensayos*, (Madrid 1975).
Mays, J.B., *Cultura adolescente en la sociedad actual* (Barcelona, 1968).
Myersblair, G. and Stewart Jones, R., *Cómo es el adolescente y cómo educarlo* (Buenos Aires 1965).